Triumphant Innocence

Walking with Jesus; True Love is Possible

To Pat
Love
Jean.
May 2012

Lottie Gillmore

TRIUMPHANT INNOCENCE
Walking with Jesus; True Love is Possible

Scripture texts in this work taken from the New American Bible with Revised New Testament and Revised Psalms © 1991, 1986, 1970 Confraternity of Christian Doctrine, Washington, D.C. are used by permission of the copyright owner. All rights reserved.

ISBN-13: 978-1-77069-443-9

Word Alive Press
131 Cordite Road, Winnipeg, MB R3W 1S1
www.wordalivepress.ca

WORD ALIVE PRESS
Just Write!

Library and Archives Canada Cataloguing in Publication

Gilmore, Lottie, 1957-
Triumphant innocence : walking with Jesus : true love is possible / Lottie Gilmore.

Includes index.
ISBN 978-1-77069-443-9

1. Love--Anecdotes. 2. Love--Religious aspects--Christianity--Anecdotes. 3. God (Christianity)--Love--Anecdotes. I. Title.

BF575.L8G55 2012   177'.7   C2011-908438-4

In Dedication

This little book of love, humour and compassion is the immediate result of my sweet husband's time spent with me over the past 22 years.

This January 2nd, 2012, my husband and I are celebrating 21 years of marriage that truly have been the best years of my entire life. Together we have walked hand in hand, with Jesus at the core of our relationship and thus have received much fruit in our lives.

I would just like to say a sincere, "Thank you, Honey, for always standing by me through thick and thin in life situations. The compassionate love you have always showered upon me has truly made me the person I am today."

GOD Bless You. May Jesus continue to lead your footsteps and lift your heart to soar. Thank you for your gentle yet strong presence in my life. GOD has made you a wonderful blessing to all that know you! Love you Sweetheart...Forever and ever.

Marriage Blessings

Long into the night...
In a dimly lit room...
We tumble...
Longing to show our love...
Whispering sweet emotions...
While feeling and touching...
Bending and stretching...
With tingling nerves...
Never before...
Has love been so deep...
Caressing with lips...
And finger tips...
Romance builds to huge proportions...
Emerging from the inside to out...
Swept up in Heavenly Love...
Before we know it...
GOD turns night into dawn.

Table of Contents

Prelude
The Truth of the Matter

As we grow older, we look back sometimes and see many wonderful events that can only be explained as being "Supernatural Miracles" from the Maker of Heaven, Himself. We daily go about our chores, duties, hobbies and pleasures, most of the time not even thinking in terms of "miracles," at least not for ourselves!

But if we have EVER asked Jesus into our hearts and even remotely try to live a faithful life in Christ, then that means our names are written in the Book of Lambs, Somewhere, way up above, in Heaven and if we are walking in the Spirit of God, we experience GOD's miraculous presence EVERY day!

Now I'd like to share with you how this love book of "Christian Romance" began in my heart and mind. How by the Grace of GOD, the Holy Spirit ignited the "fire" inside me to try to portray what I feel I have lived, since Jesus brought my sweet, tender loving yet strong, like a lion, victorious Christian husband into the deepest depth of my heart and life.

Introduction

How GOD Brought This Christian Romance Book into Being

Spring was on the end of March 2010. It was a Friday evening and the week had been very full of work, event's and just stuff. My husband had been working 12 hour days, five days a week for almost four month's so far and I seemed to be always on the run also, whether to work or to something else I deemed important.

The evening had been simple, relaxing in front of the television and in the kitchen with my computer. It soon was 10:00 o'clock p.m., when, my husband, Randall and I felt, more than ready to go to bed and conk out for the night.

We had our night clothes on, brushed our teeth, said our prayers, and like usual, snuggled together hoping to redeem our tired bodies with a good night's sleep. However, again Jesus was about to do some redirecting in our lives.

Lights out and a window was slightly open, as we were just about ready to drift into semi-consciousness, I was the recipient of the Holy Spirit's Presence.

In the still of the night, as I lay beside Randall, who was facing away from me, I, all of a sudden felt like I was in the middle of a cloud, perhaps like being a butterfly in the middle of a, cocoon. The "cloud" felt like it just sort of fell onto me from above. Next I noticed that I felt slightly squeezed, like the "cocoon" was applying gentle pressure from the outside to the inside. With this firm but gentle grip, I felt a huge compulsion to "WRITE!"

This very strong desire, I realized, was to write another book. I said out loud to Randall, who was trying to sleep, "I HAVE to write a book!" "Not just a poem, but a BOOK!" Then I stated, "But WHAT am I going to write about?" I didn't have a clue about what subject matter, so I asked my question again, this time loud enough to wake up my precious sleeping husband.

"Randall, I feel I HAVE to write another book, but what should it be about?!"

For those of you who don't know my husband, I am here to share with you that he is and for twenty years now, has always been my best friend. He always tries to meet my needs emotionally, mentally, spiritually and yes, also physically. Even when he is put on the spot, he gives me respect, tired or not tired.

Half sitting, half laying behind Randall, with this quite sincerely desperate question in his ear, he woke up, heard my question and responded with one word.

"Sex!"

Shrinking back onto my pillow, I evaluated his choice topic, and knew he was being kind, yet a bit sarcastic and really would like me to allow him to go to sleep. With just hearing Randall's choice of subject matter, I lay there quietly while the Holy Spirit covered my whole being while seemingly guiding me. As I considered the "sex" topic, I very soon realized that sex and romance are GOD given and are also very necessary in any marriage. I knew in a moment of reminiscing, in my mind that with my personal marriage experience with Randall, that romance, sex and humour are vital for a healthy, strong relationship.

Within minutes, I knew the story line of my next book and again it was to be written from truth. I tried to lie quietly and even go to sleep, but there again after a visit from GOD, I could not help myself except to get up and write!

I went to the kitchen table and there my pen poured out two pages of the start of this little "Christian Romance" book. Never in my life have I read a "romance" book, but by the Grace of our Living Saviour, I have been given a man that is GODLY, loving, kind, funny and Mr. Romance himself.

And to this day, twenty years later, that fire of affection in two young adults still is FULL of humour, empathy, desire and passion!

A few details of life that I believe are true in an abundant meaningful, successful marriage are:

1) A woman needs her husband to be her best friend, emotionally and physically, while,

2) A man needs his wife to be his lover and best friend.

3) And Jesus needs to be at the center of it all.

With Jesus at the lead of this story, I am inviting you to get a tall hot drink, wet your lips, sink into a comfortable easy chair and enjoy my story of untold Guppy Love that the GREAT LOVER HIMSELF, GOD of the Universe, orchestrated in my life.

Chapter One
Way Back When

Alone in the car, the black night veil covered the still, warm air. I, Elizabeth, sat, lonely, hurting, waiting and waiting, while a small still voice in the center of my 30 year old Christian woman's heart cried silently out to my invisible God. With my wheelchair bound mother taken up to her apartment, groceries carried to my mother's small abode, for a few quiet, still moments, I, verbally called out to my living life saving Saviour, Jesus of Nazareth.

"Jesus, oh precious Jesus!"

Looking directly from a sitting position in the driver's seat into the bare passenger seat, I felt the Holy Presence of the very Jesus that had saved me from death's doorway only three years earlier.

"Please... Jesus, help me...Jesus!!"

"Jesus...What now! What do I do now!! Please help me!! What do I have to do to meet a best friend husband that will love me for me! What do I have to do to meet a loving Christian man that has the same heart as I? Who has God in the middle of his heart, like my heart?"

"Who will love me for my heart!! Not for my car. Not for my job. Not for my money or my looks!"

"GOD, I will NOT go to a bar to look for a man and take part in that meat market! NO!"

"Precious Jesus, please send me a Christian man who will be my best friend first, then possibly, my husband".

As I sat motionless crying out to God in my still dark car, I looked in my rear view mirror, starring through salty tears at the bar, lounge building next to my mother's high rise apartment.

Tears streaming down my cheeks uncontrollably, I blurted out my hearts horrible pain of loneliness along with deep, hopeful desires. Little did I know it; but Jesus was there that late, dark night's conversation, in that solo atmosphere...agreeing to meet my sincerest heart's desires.

Tears dried and purpose refocused, I started my 1976 Ford Cougar, parked the old car in one of the visitors apartment parking spaces, locked my doors and hurriedly headed to my mom's suite, ten stories above ground. The heavy emotional weight that numbed my body was once again pressure relieved, at least for now. Tears were good. Talking to Jesus was great. But laying this painful burden at the foot of the Cross was even better.

Maybe now I could relax enough to have a decent night's sleep, with my quiet, loving mother gently sleeping right there in the next room.

Many evenings, after taking mother grocery shopping, I would sit mummified, numb and unresponsive to sight, sound or feelings, like that in a state of an up-right comma. Alive, but not alive! Breathing, but not breathing. I was numb, not feeling. Eyes open, yet oblivious to any surroundings. By the Grace of GOD, my mind, body and soul was temporarily put into overdrive, perhaps automatic GOD Co-pilot.

Week after week, the modest Friday evenings and nights, at my mother's dwelling, were the same responses to a time of marriage separation and evolving divorce. The pain was like that of a death of half of my emotional body, depression and worry tearing me apart, limb from body. Would my two young boy's be cared for. Are they suffering unbearably from this divorce? Where was I and my children going to reside, and, on what income.

Chapter Two
Faithfull Truths

For literally months of tortured silent waiting, not knowing the outcome, I, Elizabeth, kept my Jesus close to my heart and mind. I knew GOD's precious word from scripture, but now GOD was showing me in "real life" what exactly His Word means.

I remembered parts of His Holy word saying: "No trial has come to you but what is human. God is faithful and will not let you be tried beyond your strength; but with the trial he will also provide a way out, so that you may be able to bear it" (1 Cor 10:13). "For God did not give us a spirit of cowardice but rather of power and love and self-control" (2 Tim 1:7). "I am the way and the truth and the life" (John 14:6). "I will never forsake you or abandon you" (Hebrews 13:5). "Peace I leave with you; my peace I give to you" (John 14:27).

And by the Grace of GOD, every Friday night, after returning from grocery shopping, for about an hour, GOD would again put my frail, skinny, emotionally torn body into that coma-like state, resting and possibly healing any damage done from the stress.

Chapter Three
Time Marches On

January came, January went. February came, February went. March had little change, but come April the unconscious depression was starting to lift. GOD's Holy Spirit was once again stirring my heart, giving me some new direction.

As GOD would have it, the moment of my seeming-less endless aching divorce situation, made a deep cut of opposite direction at the point of that intimate, desperate, yet honest conversation with Jesus, that late April, Friday night in my old Ford, outside my mother's apartment.

GOD's Word say's "Seek and ye shall find, Ask and ye shall receive, Knock and it shall open."

With GOD's Word in my heart and mind, the next four months were full of my children, my children's school and my mother's presence. Money was getting low, actually very low and trusting my Saviour for finances was getting harder and harder to do, but with GOD's Grace, I did. With macaroni and cheese meals, little gas money, uncertainty hanging heavily over our heads, I and my children felt the Peace that only GOD could give. I knew Jesus loved me right from the beginning of my, so far, short, eventful life.

In the month of June, I and my two young boys were down to the last $100.00 in my bank account which was suppose to cover food, lodging, gas, and clothing. With no-where to go, I had no alternative than to approach the low income housing and welfare agency. Up until this time I was living in the divorce home but the divorce was soon finalizing and I had to find accommodations soon, for my home was being sold. The money would be divided almost three ways, with my share the least portion.

Bye the Grace of GOD, the low rental housing staff felt and saw my strife therefore in one month, half of a duplex was available to me because they had put my name on an emergency list. With no money funds, no food, or available shelter for our small family, this available half of a duplex, was the start of many miracles to unfold. Again, I felt GOD's comforting presence.

Many well known Theologians have stated: "When we can't see what God is up to, we can trust that God is up to something very wonderfully good, working behind the scenes, for us, His precious children."

Chapter Four
Getting into the Groove

The month's of July and August somehow quickly passed. The kid's and I, were trying to get ready for another school year, this time with me as a mother first, then starting September 1989, also as a College student. My unemployment agent, back in February of 1989, enrolled me into a course of "Office Technology" and I was scheduled for the next two years of my life to attend school, which the Government paid the tuition for. The Government also paid me a wage of $400.00 a month living allowance which I was scheduled to start receiving the coming September course, come this fall.

GOD didn't give me lots of money to live on, but He did make my expenses less so that, on $400.00, I was able to still take care of my precious children. For example, an apartment basement suite cost in most places $400.00 in 1989 and my cost of that half-duplex home, with two bathrooms and three bedrooms, was only $97.00 a month, Praise our Living Jesus!

My two little boy's Mackenzie and Kirby, seemed to be fairing emotionally "ok" as I had been attending along-side them during the last four months of the previous school year. I, Elizabeth, did not want my children to have a fear of possible abandonment of me, their mother, because possibly they felt abandonment of their father and that was horrible enough.

Tearing myself and children from this loveless husband and wife set up, was up to now the hardest thing I had ever done in my whole life and now seemed the only way that I thought I could save my life and possibly my children's lives, from a life of negativity, unbelief in Jesus and possibly, even early death. I did not have the emotional or physical strength to stand up or fight for my life but I did have growing Faith in the "Rock" of "Jesus" and "The Truth of His Light."

Since I had given my heart and life to the Lord three years earlier, He had placed many timely, Supernatural Miracles within those, hard short years. With my mouth "shut" and my mind and heart focused on "Jesus," I marched forward, day by day. Every now and again, a bright light moment would present itself and again I would feel the Lord's wonderful Presence.

Little did I know, but Jesus was truly working His amazing Glory, for me, behind the scenes and soon, that Glory would present itself! By the Grace of GOD, I too would come to be a recipient of first hand, respect, laughter, kindness, romance, compassion and even true love!

Thank you to the Creator of the world!!

Chapter Five
Our New Home!

August 21, 1989, had arrived and the day to pick up our house key had come. The house had been cleaned from top to bottom for us and on September 1, we were to be the new residents!

For the last month, my children and I had rented a two bedroom, dungy apartment basement suite that had been about 400 sq. Feet. Now we were so glad for our new surroundings! We were above ground. We had two very large front-room windows, one in the dining room and the other in the living room. With a small, well designed kitchen, pantry and all, over time, I cooked many wiener, macaroni and cheese meals.

By GOD's design there were two nice sized bedrooms on the main floor, a linen closet and also a fair sized bathroom.

This being an enormous miracle for us at this time, I was also scheduled to inherit a planting of "Guppy Love" through one of GOD's chosen people. That miracle being the exact man that Jesus picked out for me and sent to me, through that prayer in my car, of last April evening. This very large miracle in my life took place on Saturday, September 21, at a supper-time meal. The dark emotional hell in my life was lifting from my shoulders and pure bright sunshine was ebbing slowly but surely, more and more frequently, from hopelessness into a life of hope.

It was the middle of September, as my boy's were settling into their new school year and I into my new college calendar school year also. I had started to receive my $400.00 monthly school allowance so I purchased two sets of dusty rose louvers for our two large windows. We had to have privacy from the main roadway out front. I was able to find and buy a second hand floor area carpet for the living room. We had our old table and chairs set and our old black and yellow couch set. When the louvers were put up and the furniture put into place, "Wow!", I liked our new home even better than our old family home. Maybe it was because Jesus was welcomed into our new home and His love shone brightly from every corner!

The house was looking great when I received a telephone call from a dear friend. She said her husband was going out of town for the third weekend of September and she thought I was ready to meet a man friend of hers, maybe over supper, in her home. Well, I was kind of surprised to hear that my friend thought I was READY but somehow I thought, it couldn't hurt. I was lonely.

I knew in every fibre of my being that any man that I would date HAD to have Jesus in the middle of his heart. GOD had to prevail in the life of my "Mr. Right."

The finalisation date of my divorce was quickly approaching as it was set for October 1, 1989, and the blind supper date was set for September 21, less than ten day before then.

With rattled nerves and very high wall reservations about the whole coming evening, time just kept ticking and I just kept on praying and believing GOD's Word. I accepted the invitation, trusting, hoping and maybe just a little bit, expecting GOD to do a little more rebuilding in my once torn, shattered life, like HIS Word says.

Chapter Six
Would Mr. Right Please Stand Up?

All nervous and jittery, emotional walls towering high, on every side of me, for now the big blind date evening had arrived! The boy's had been scheduled to visit their father for the weekend and it was now or possibly, never, to talk to a member of the opposite sex. I questioned myself. Did I look ok...Was I dressed ok...Did I smell ok... Then I calmly addressed my concerns by telling myself, "It's only a supper" and "I'm going into "Friendly" territory. Come on now, Elizabeth, pull your boots straps up. Do the right thing and at least give this guy a chance! Chill, watch, listen and trust your Lord!"

Before leaving our house, one more quick prayer was on my lips and as I remember, it went something like this, "Dear GOD, if this guy is not Mr. Right, please show me. Let me know, somehow!"

Remembering from where I had come from in my past marriage, not to mention the physiological and emotional pain of my childhood, I really didn't want to repeat the same mistake, not now or EVER again! I knew in my new heart, that GOD had recently given to me that HE also wanted to give me a healthy, loving life and that might include a loving, Christian man especially chosen by my Maker, just for me.

Prayer said, car started, I ventured out into my evening of the unknown. When I pulled up to my friends home, again the anxious and jittering nerves were doing their thing. I literally shook like a leaf. I rang the door bell and took a very deep breath and tried to shake off the fear.

Edna, my long life, dear friend greeted me with a great big smile and confidence. She showed me up the stairs and there was Mr. Mystery. He looked fine. Not dangerous or anything. He also wore a smile and decent clothes. Other than that I don't remember much else of his style, all though I seem to remember that a lot of our three-some conversation was all about hockey, hockey and more hockey. GOD knows that hockey is a very big sport in Canada and even though I am born and raised, Canadian, I am in NO way, shape or form, now or have ever supported "hockey." I actually dislike it quite a bit because of the violence and possible injury to the players and even sometimes the fans. I guess it's the fighting of hockey that I dislike so much. The game itself is fast and interesting.

Even, with that conversation topic on the table, I in my nervousness and trying to be pleasant, wasn't aware of "hockey" possibly being a, "red flag."

Supper smelled delicious, all though, again I don't remember what the menu was. After small talk for a about fifteen minutes with this nice, yet complete stranger and my girl friend, it was time to get to the table. Now my wonderful friend, bless her heart, is not a religious woman, but she is a sincere, loving and caring friend and for some reason was about to speak GOD right into the evening!

Up until now, any evidence of RED flags was mild and supper was on.

21

Each of us finding our seats, we sat down quickly and quietly, when out of Edna's mouth came the words, "Elizabeth, would you say Grace, please?"

Completely dumbstruck and surprised, I did as asked. Never before had any of my friends asked me to pray over a meal in their home. True, my faith in Jesus had become the most important element of my life and I did sometimes pray over my meals at home, but publicly praying with strangers present, up until now, had never transpired!

Spiritually put on the spot, I asked the Lord's blessings on our meal, the company and that HE bless us for the evening.

WOW! Almost instantly, the whole atmosphere around the table became VERY cold. It was as if a bucket of ice cold water was poured right into our laps. The conversation was strained. The nice young stranger man became almost speechless, stumbling for conversation. Since, Edna's friend couldn't just get up and leave, we politely finished our dinner and retrieved to the living room.

Within literally, after ten minutes of assembling after supper, my mystery man, graciously informed Edna and I that he had to take his son to hockey and he was GONE! Jesus knew his heart and Jesus knew my heart, and apparently our hearts did not match.

I do believe that GOD definitely has a sense of humour and when we pray, HE hears. Praise GOD! HE was also teaching me to EXPECT to receive an ANSWER and I did!

Within minutes of, mystery man number one, exiting Edna's and my company, romance was once again raising to possibilities. Edna, I believe was on a mission, maybe instructed by GOD Himself because as the door closed behind "Mr. Hockey night in Canada," "Mr. Mystery" number two's name was revealed into our conversation.

I couldn't believe my ears! Edna was bound and determined to now introduce me to yet another single man she knew! There had been no warning for this poor fellow, of any new introductions to a woman and now at 8:00 p.m. on a Saturday night, Edna was about to make a surprise telephone call to Randall Soffit. Maybe, Randall would be home and maybe, just maybe, he would like to come see two women that he only knew of in passing, for pie and ice cream.

Agreeing to Edna's suggestion, the call was put into operation. As I sat there listening to my end of the conversation, I heard the invite, some persuading and explaining and finally, something that sounded like an agreement to attend our little tea party.

When Edna got off of the telephone, she explained to me that, yes, Randall had just got home, was getting ready to go to bed and hesitantly, had decided to come over.

For the next half hour or so, we waited and chatted while Edna explained to me that this gentleman actually was a lot like me. She previously had not said that about man number one, but this time was reassuring me that Randall and I had many similarities. She told me that, like me, he had two children. He had been divorced for about five years already. He was very kind. He was in the Auto Body industry and was a hard worker. And he also went to church regularly, like me!

When I heard that statement, my ears immediately perked up!

Again my heart's desire to meet a loving Christian man was brought to the front burner. Maybe, just maybe, this was the man that Jesus had plans for me to get to know. But even still, I had staggering, tall emotional walls, standing strongly all around me, just in case more daggers where coming my way. I knew that whomever Jesus was going to send, he had to prove himself to me, as worthy. It wouldn't be what he looked like or what he drove that would decide yes or no for me, actually I didn't care even about his finances. I just knew that he had to have a loving heart and GOD is love.

While Edna seemed very enthusiastic about the whole meeting, there was one thing that Edna seemed unsure of, and that was when she questioningly and almost apologizing mentioned to me that he was however "Catholic." I didn't know what to think about that, except that I believed in ONE GOD, ONE JESUS, and ONE HOLY SPIRIT, no matter what the denomination. Again, I turned my faith to GOD, waited and trusted.

Now after twenty years plus.., Randall and I still chuckle about that once mentioned "Catholic" concern, Praise GOD!

Soon there was a light knock on the front door. He was here. Oh, my Gosh, round number two!

Edna let Randall in with a sincere greeting, while I sat motionless on the couch, waiting and watching with ears and eyes wide open. As the two of them walked up the stairs into the living room, I noticed right away that he was a good height, that being taller than me. His face was very gentle looking and his speech was firm but soft with his vivid blue eyes being very piercing.

As I got up off the couch, he approached me as he extended out his right hand. Hand in hand, we touched, while looking deeply into each other's eyes. His grip was firm, solid and yet smooth and inviting. He said "Hello," as I did the same.

Taking our places on the couches, Edna sat on the love seat placed between our chairs. Coffee and pie was served as somehow conversation seemed to roll off of our lips. Judging and testing EVERY-THING he said, the evening was way too soon over! He was a perfect gentleman! He had manors! He had respect for his mother and women! He was funny and gentle as he looked me right in the eyes for communication. GOD was present in this man's heart! Yes, with his sincere smile and bright eyes he made a very strong, good, lasting impression on me!

With my thoughts racing I thought, "Dear Jesus, could this be "Mr. Right." With the clock ticking, the evening was starting to close. The last two hours had flown by and I don't really remember what all we talked about, but it was good. Now it was time that Randall, Edna and I said our "Good nights."

We walked back down the steps to the front door, while getting our shoes on. Then Randall turned to me, again extended his right hand and gently but firmly squeezed warmth into the palm of my hand, and said, "It was really nice to meet you, Elizabeth. May I call you sometime... soon?"

Again I noticed his stature. I was looking up-wards into his handsome facial features, blue eyes and contoured lips.

As my heart seemed to melt, I could only answer, "Yes, please do. I would like that."

Together we left the house and proceeded to our own vehicles. The mystery evening was over and somehow I held a warm, fuzzy feeling somewhere deep inside the somewhat melting emotional walls. Yes, this was good.

Chapter Seven
A Gem in the Rough

Mackenzie, Kirby and I into our second month of schooling, it seemed the emotional stress in our lives was lessening. We were settling into our new home, new school classes and new lives.

It had been a couple of weeks since Randall and I had met. I still had not had a phone call from him plus I didn't know if I was going to get one. I was not into phoning men, first of all because I didn't know any and secondly, it just wasn't in me to be the assertive one, so I put it on the back burner of my life, prayed and waited.

Now Edna was a creature of a different motto. She was assertive. She did call Randall. Not just once, but a few times over that two week waiting period. For the whole evening with us at her house, she sat totally glued to our conversation. She never interrupted, but mentally took down each word and meaning. She could barely stand to leave us alone for five minutes while she made her way to the wash room.

Randall, I found out later, had actually circled Edna's house block three times before inching his way to Edna's front door that first evening meeting. In his mind, he had after five years of being single, decided to raise his two children first before seeking another life partner. What he was seeking in a man and woman relationship, he thought was very rare, because of the couples he saw around himself.

In the midst of singleness, broken hearts, bitterness and searching men and women, there was, however, one couple that Randall was friends with that shone of love and genuine caring. In Randall's mind, that was what he wanted for a relationship with the woman of his dreams.

The calls from Edna to Randall, actually almost ended any further interaction between Randall and me. Randall was somewhat interested in me, but he was not about to go into another relationship where a woman was going to push him around. By receiving so many inquiring phone calls from Edna, that emotional control and force almost pushed him right out of my big, life picture.

Randall also informed me, at a later time that he had met another young woman just weeks before me, whom was from another city close by. She also was waiting for him to come see her.

For some unknown reason, I believe GOD had his hand on Randall. Randall cancelled his future meeting with the woman in Lethbridge, and decided to call me instead. Randall had so many decisions to make and like all the other decisions, this also was to play a major role in his life, and mine.

Finally after a two week wait, my phone rang. There was no such thing as call waiting, answering machines or telephone I.D., so just like every other time it rang, I just answered it. With great surprise and awe, I answered the man's voice on the other end with, "This is she," to learn that possible "Mr. Right," Randall Soffit, was on the line!

It seemed uncanny, that even after two weeks had passed by since we last had talked; our conversation was again full and detailed. His interest in me seemed sincere, while I could hear and feel his gentleness. Before I knew it, almost an hour had flown by, and we were saying our "Goodbyes" and again he asked me if he could call me again soon.

I couldn't believe my ears! He wanted to get to know me better. He agreed with almost all of my Christian opinions of life, that I felt comfortable to share so far with him. He didn't think I was stupid for my "Faith" opinions. He actually inquired of some of my beliefs on general things and agreed, in his soft demeanour, with just about everything I commented on. I had been judging him by what was coming out of his mouth, which I believe was coming out of his heart. This, Randall Soffit, was a man of GOD and I knew almost right away that where GOD resided, great happiness resided also.

The thick, high walls of emotional protection around me were being softened and emotions within me showed signs of "melting" the iron stone barriers. I didn't want to run ahead of Jesus, but I did want to trust HIM and follow closely as HE lead.

Like I had prayed, five months previously, I had asked Jesus for a man that would love me for my heart. I didn't care what kind of car he drove or if he had lots of money in the bank. I asked GOD for a best friend to share my life and my children's lives. I was praying for a man that had Jesus also, inside his heart and life.

Please GOD, give me someone that has compassion, empathy, joy, peace, tenderness, self-control and gives with a cheerful heart, someone that would include me and my children in the circle of GOD's LOVE.

Chapter Eight
¾ Turkey Bird

For the month of October, 1989, I was the recipient of many wonderful multi-detailed conversations with this incredibly hearted man. In my thirty two years of life, I had never known many men and I certainly had never known any man so much like myself. This was a man that actually talked with me, about anything that came to mind, whether religion, education, health, our kid's, our ex-spouses, right and wrong issues and GOD's WORD was always the anchor for our reasoning.

With our conversation's I noticed that Randall was full of forgiveness. He held no bitterness towards his fellow man or previous wife. His heart was overflowing with life, love, romance and humour. Together we were a picture of material poverty, but spiritually, with GOD's presence, we were very rich!

After a few of our wonderful conversation's via telephone, I invited Randall to drop by for a visit on a Friday evening, thus started our very slow going commitment to each other. During the weekday's, my two beautiful boy's and myself would attend school, while Randall would carry on with his work routine as an auto body mechanic.

Soon every evening after all the kid's had gone to bed, the phone line would light up again and another hour or so would be talked late into the night. Very rapidly, Randall was proving to me that a man could be my best friend.

Talking and talking, October flew by very quickly and November was upon us. Randall also played hockey in the winter time with his buddies, the White Foxes, and very soon I was to be initiated into, "The Hockey Kitchen of Turkey Fame!"

There was going to be a hockey tournament, followed by a somewhat large evening meal. All the hockey players decided to ask their spouse or other half to help cook the celebrating supper of the hockey event.

So it came to pass that Randall decided to ask me if I would cook the turkey bird that he was assigned to, after all we were becoming a budding team. All I was told was that he would bring me the bird and I could cook it in my oven. Now I had never been much of a cook, except for macaroni and cheese and other simple menus, but after all, he took sincere interest in me so what harm could there be in returning the gesture. It might even be fun! Maybe I could even prove to myself and Randall that I am a great little cook!

The day's kept unfolding, as our conversations kept us both intrigued and intensely satisfied. Finally the big hockey weekend tournament was here and low and behold the door bell rang. I was greeted at my front door by Randall and in his arms was a bag with the largest turkey bird inside it that looked like it could feed a small army.

He lugged it inside and carried it to the kitchen, put it in the sink, breathed a sigh of relief and said, "There you go, Elizabeth...Have at her. It's all yours!"

Previously, I had told Randall that I owned a roaster pan that was over sized and all should be ok.

However, now I was not so sure! After Randall left for the hockey rink, I dug out the roaster, wiped it down and tried to place the huge bird inside. The bird was definitely the biggest turkey I had ever seen, let alone had ever tried to cook. So with great diligence I literally squeezed and stuffed it into the pan the best I could. Actually, I'm not sure that it wasn't an old ostrich bird and it was going to try to fight me all the way!

The stupid thing took ten packages of dressing and still there was room for more. It's wings and legs draped far outside of the pan, so I just knew there would be "smoke," and the lid, well, therefore, that was NOT able to close the bird tightly inside either.

With me being an inexperienced cook, I mulled over the idea of "How long do I cook this thing." I didn't want to send people home sick with eating over done, dry or worse yet, raw meat! I just couldn't believe my eyes but I knew that now the challenge was on! GOD, help me!

With the big bird stuffed and seasoned, into the regular sized oven it went. I did not know what really would happen with its leg's and wing's sticking out, but in it went anyways. The oven was heated to 400F and so I waited.

I had gone down stairs to do some laundry, when the sound of a screeching smoke alarm riveted throughout the entire house. Was the house on "Fire!" I dropped everything and raced up the stairs while grey smoke made its way "thicker and thicker" around me as I approached the kitchen oven.

I knew instantly that this big dumb bird was dripping grease from its extremities and my oven didn't like it!

Very quickly, I turned the oven off and then opened the oven door with the smoke only emitting more. Running to the side door of the duplex, I opened the door as wide as possible, then, I ran back to the oven to turn on the stove fan! The whole time my ears were being pierced by the fire alarm "screaming" loudly for me and for all to hear!

Out loudly I mumble something about, "Great Scott!!!" "Randall!!!" "Randall!!!" "What a Stupid Bird!!!"

As I got a big towel and started to wave it frantically, like there was a great wind, I aimed it upwards towards the ceiling alarm, with panic praying for silence and peace.

I guess I wasn't the perfect little cook after all and returning the love gesture really was a "challenge."

About an hour after the "working alarm system" signal, the house air was fairly clear again. When I returned to the area of the aggravated turkey bird, I did some adjusting, like taking a sharp, large knife and proceeded to cut the legs and wings right off.

Apparently, I didn't have a pan to fit the turkey, so I made the turkey fit the pan. After wiping out the oven, I put the "three quarter" bird back in the oven, closed the door and once again turned the stove on. This time success was in the air and by late evening we had a very nicely browned cooked bird, whatever kind it was. Thank you Jesus! Yes, I think I had just been initiated by Randall Soffit!

Looking back, I don't even remember the banquet evening supper very much, but by the Grace of GOD, that bird was consumed and no one that I am aware of, got sick. Again, thank you, Precious Saviour.

Chapter Nine
Tea Towels and Things

Life was good. The children were coping with school, divorce, schedules and our meagre finances. They were accepting my new man friend, and Randall seemed to accept them. The four of us spent many meals together and outside activities, like biking, hockey, and soccer etc.

The months rolled from October to November, then November to December, while our family's personal bonding became evident. Randall was so good with the boys. He cared for them like they were his own. His compassion for both me and my children was very strong. One thing that was very important to me was also that the Christian man that may come into my life, also HAD to love my boy's. We were a package deal and that's all there was to it, after all, my divorce was also for my children, because I loved them so much!

One Saturday supper meal, we had just finished a satisfying menu that was simple but delicious. Randall as always, was a perfect gentleman. The boy's were excused from the table while I went to the kitchen sink to run water for the dishes. Randall started to clear the table as we chatted about the week's events.

Sink full of dish water. Dishes being washed by me and dried by Randall, we were completing our tasks. Sometime half way finished, with wet hands, I turned around to face Randall, who had a tea towel in hand, saw his gentle face and all of a sudden his arms were around my upper body. He leaned towards me, gave me a sweet kiss with a long, warm hug when silently and quite accidentally, my bra unhooked! The look on my face was one of GREAT surprise and then when I told him what had just happened, he too had a sheepish grin of surprise also.

Moments later, when we both realized what had just transpired, we couldn't stop laughing! It was so funny for a few reasons. First of all, so far, our intimacy was only one of beautiful conversation. Our bonding had been emotional up until now, which was about two months of talking and friendship, and now in one kiss and hug, it seemed I was accidentally getting undressed, from the inside out!

Never before or since has my bra popped undone by being hugged, thank goodness! Maybe this was one of GOD's ways of drawing us even closer, I don't know. I do know that GOD does have a sense of humour and HE sometimes mixes it with romance.

Christmas came and Christmas went, while Randall and I continued to emotionally get closer and closer. Our bond of friendship was starting to sprout strong deep roots.

Four months, after we started seeing each other, my walls of emotional protection had become very soft and were withering. I found myself very much in love with this caring, gentle, yet strong man. I loved how he looked, talked, moved, ate, thought and especially how he put me on some kind of special pedestal. He always respected me. He allowed me to be me. I didn't have to be the best cook or have the best career job. I didn't have to own the perfect car or have bundles of money at my disposal. He showed that he cared for my heart, my spiritual beliefs and loved me for my "simplicity" and honesty. Praise GOD for answered prayers! GOD is GOOD!

Then one Friday evening in the middle of January, when my children were staying the night at their fathers, it happened. Randall and I became physical. I couldn't believe how my heart soared and raced with the tenderness of when his touches became reality. GOD only knows how hungry my entire being was for such compassion and physical touch. I knew it was wrong, but we were so thirsty for each other's bodies, we were completely helpless to fight against it.

All the time, in the moment of love making, Randal would keep asking me, "Are you sure?" "Are you sure?"

All the time, while melting into his arms, I knew I loved him with all my soul and heart, so conceded to accepting and enjoying his advances.

Our physical romance was however soon cut short because as a praying Christian, within the next couple of weeks, I was visited by a vision of our Lord, Jesus.

I did know that premarital sex was totally wrong! I KNEW it, but was weak, so that is, when sleeping in my own bed by my-self, Jesus came down from Heaven, to give me moral strength and wisdom.

Lying in my bed, eyes closed but half awake, there He was, Jesus, coming down from the ceiling above me in my bed! He was floating there above me, coming down closer and closer to me, so that I could see Him motioning His head from side to side, telling me, NO to sex. Since GOD had saved me from spiritual and physical death and sickness, supernaturally, only a few years earlier, I KNEW again that He was intervening again very supernaturally.

Therefore this vision also meant everything to me! Jesus was directing my life's path and I knew I had to "Stop" this very electrifying physical behaviour. I had learned to "trust" Jesus.

The next visit with Randall, I had no choice, I had to share with him the vision GOD gave me. I was so worried that he may think that I was crazy, ungrateful of his love or that I was actually trying to push him away! None of that was true! I loved this dear sweet man! I could only do what I knew Jesus wanted me to do and that was cut off the sex. I cried out in private, "Jesus; please help Randall accept my decision to love him without total physical contact, at least for now!"

By the Mercy of GOD, Randall's reaction again was one of total respect for me. I'm sure that many men, that had the taste of sexual relations with a woman, then turned away, would literally turn and run as fast as their legs would take them, in the opposite direction. This however was not the case with Randall. The man of my dreams... loved me.

I had never in my life been the recipient of such love by another person, let alone a man. I knew then that GOD definitely had put this diamond of a Christian man into my life for reasons that were so good, words cannot describe. The faithfulness and complete loving of another person, I had never known before. Now I was on the trail of truly finding out that this was the beginning of love in the deepest form. Only GOD would know how far reached Randall's and my love would develop, because "GOD is LOVE" and now, He was showering me with it! Glory Be to GOD!

We had just known each other for a few months when the evidence of Randall's compassion and morals, started to shower me with selfless compassion and enduring love.

*   ★   ★   ★

Coming to town was an Elvis Impersonator show, that for some reason my friends wanted me to attend with them. I didn't have much money but with my new found marriage freedom, I decided to squeeze in the ticket price as part of my monthly expense. I had never been to an Elvis Impersonator, and I really wanted to celebrate my independence with my two dear friends, so the tickets were bought.

Not once did I think that Randall may like to take me for a rare night outs event. As soon as my friends had asked me to attend the show with them, I decided to share this eventful news with Randall.

I guess I must have sounded excited about the girl's night out, because Randall, without any hesitation, agreed with me that it could be a very enjoyable evening out with the girls, for me.

It was almost a year later that I learned that my sweet Randall, a year earlier, had bought two tickets, one for him and one for me, for the Elvis show. He bought them before I told him that my friends wanted me to attend with them.

Randall was financially not well to do, but he sacrificed the ticket money to please me. He bought two tickets for us, to be a surprise. He had the tickets before I decided to buy one. He gracefully empowered me to buy my ticket and like the prince he is, he stepped aside of the whole evening. I still don't know if he was able to return the tickets or what became of them. All I know is that, already at that time of our relationship, Randall loved me enough to put my desires first, before his.

Like GOD's Word say's, "His eyes are on the sparrow," and Randall also had his "hearts eyes" on me, his sparrow.

Talking, caring, interacting and building our relationship continued while full veins of life ran freely between us. In only months, it felt like we had been friends for most of our lives and soon a dedication of commitment, was pouring from our hearts.

The months seemed to fly by effortlessly. Our respect and conversation moulded into something that I believe every person yearns for and only "sometimes" get. Randall had proven his love for me by agreeing to my, "no sex" decision and now we both were falling hard and deeply into a "Guppy Love."

Chapter Ten
When We Get Married

It was Easter time and beauty was all around us, inside and outside. Our children were almost finished another school year and I was almost finished my first College year. We had just settled down for a late movie on TV. Supper finished, boy's in bed and us sitting closely on the couch, another perfect moment was about to penetrate the still calm atmosphere.

While in quiet conversation, Randall, full of mischief and boyish charm, all of a sudden, blurted uncontrollably. "When we get married" and then onto other details of our lives. He cupped my hand, his eye's smiling a questioning smile with brilliant blue eyes, looking directly and deeply into my green eyes, and then waited. I had not been expecting a proposal and was taken off guard, when after a few moments of that comment soaking into me, I giggled and replied, "Did you just propose to me, Randall?" Without any reservation he said, "Yes."

I looked out into the kitchen for a brief moment and then back to my very special friend. With a love like I have never felt before, I didn't have to think too long on my decision because I knew from the get go, that "Mr. Right" was sitting right next to me. I knew that with Jesus as our director, our marriage was being sowed into fertile soil.

I knew he was serious, and I knew I loved him, so without any hesitation I also answered, "Yes!"

We leaned into each other as Randall stroked my curly brown hair and gently kissed me on the lips. I had no idea how "right" this little word, "Yes," decision was, but I knew that I truly enjoyed every moment of his presence and I didn't ever want my "Prince Charming" to leave.

The day's and night's kept melting into the spring and finally, summer. Soon school and college were over for us, for the year and I was still patiently waiting for evidence of an engagement ring. On the wonderful event of being proposed to, Randall had explained to me that "soon" he would surprise me with a visit to the Jeweller's.

A couple of month's had passed, when finally, when I least expected it, Randall set up a date with me for a whole warm, July, fun day in the park. However, the day was planned for just Randall and I, and I just felt in my spirit, that something good was up.

Early on July 18, 1990, I heard a loud knock, with a little bit of singing, at my front door. My boy's had stayed over at their dad's the night before and I was anticipating a romantic day in the park with my husband to be. Randall seemed to beam as I let him in the door. He had on an ironed pair of jeans and tailored short sleeved shirt. His shoes were shined and today, his eyes were especially vivid blue.

As he danced around me like a butterfly, commenting on how beautiful I looked, I soaked up his excitement. He said he wanted to take me out to a special luncheon on his motorcycle and I could pick "The Place." First I gave him a cheek to cheek big hug, and then gathered my purse, sandals, a light sweater and we were off.

In my opinion, of motorcycles, driving them wasn't very safe because I had always thought them to have little or no protection so therefore, could be quite dangerous. But Randall was not only always caring for me as a gentleman but also took great care in his driving habits with me on his motorcycle. He didn't want to scare me in any way, shape or form so he drove fairly slowly with no show-boating. Actually, I felt quite safe and comfortable, but only with him!

The traffic wasn't too heavy this early in the day and now we were heading for my favourite dinner spot, that being the White Spot Restaurant, where the food was superior to most. Lunch like usual, was divine and the atmosphere with my Romeo, couldn't have been sweeter.

Lunch time over, we were back in the motorcycle saddle and we were off for downtown. I didn't know exactly where we were going, but still, Randall was beaming like a school kid with his hand in a candy jar. With the wind blowing briskly against our bodies, we stopped our ride outside one of Medicine Hat's downtown's well know jewellery stores. Once we were stopped, my attentive driver, got off the bike, helped me off the bike and once again brought my attention to "engagement rings."

"Now Elizabeth, I love you with all my heart and if you will marry me you will make me the happiest man on Earth. I know I am not wealthy with money and I know I can't afford expensive things right now, but I will always LOVE YOU with ALL my heart! I will treat you like my princess all the days of my life, if you only become my beloved bride."

His sincerity and charm warmed me from the very core of my being. I knew, so far in my whole life, that he was the most incredible caring, GODLY hearted man I had ever met. I felt his genuine "Guppy Love" and his empathy of what my GODLY Grandmother, Louis, always called "Real." There was only tenderness and truth in his words and in his words were also actions... Jesus was, right at the moment, answering my earlier sincere prayer conversation that took place a year earlier, in the late of the night, within my old car.

Standing on the sidewalk in front of Randall, with tears of over whelming joy running down my cheeks, I didn't know how to respond, as I was melting from the inside out, except to whisper, "I love you so, so much! I want to be your wife...You are my best friend!"

He gently leaned into me, wrapped his strong arms around my quivering shoulders, kissed me on the lips and whispered into my ear, "Honey, let's go buy you a ring!"

Again, my heart was doing flip flops, as we entered the house of diamonds.

Chapter Eleven
Ring on My Finger

With in an hour's time of shopping, we emerged from the jewellery store, once more to straddle Randall's motorcycle. For this ride however, Randall now carried in his leather jacket pocket a modest but beautiful gold wedding ring set. It was a small solitaire diamond gold engagement band with a matching smaller gold wedding band. For Randall's and my wedding bands, we choose two matching wider gold wedding bands with a small diamond chip on each.

Randall had been saving his money for this special day, for months and now our day was here!

Back in the saddle and we were off! Again, I didn't know where my "Prince Charming" was taking me but I soon would find out.

As we sped through the, now increasing, downtown traffic, I could hardly wait for the next surprise! In and out of passing trucks and cars, the wind blew gingerly against our faces and bodies. Happiness and excitement filled me to the brim!

While riding on the motorcycle, Randall and I were never able to speak to each other, so I just hung on tightly to the man I was soon going to marry, all the while grinning excitingly from ear to ear. Actually, I probably appeared, to passing people, like I had just "stolen" something very valuable and was now trying to make a fast get away, looking to dispense of the evidence!

I couldn't help notice that we were heading for an area of Medicine Hat that I hardly ever passed through and soon we were near the train tracks. In the middle of nowhere almost, there in front of us was a lovely city park, gazebo, stone wall entrance and pink and yellow flowers, all in the setting of a quiet, serene, beautiful garden.

Stopping the bike, we without hesitation, jumped off. Randall then embedded my eager hand into his large, warm palm and led me, without a word to the gazebo in the middle of the park. Now, together as we stood motionless, looking deeply into each other's eyes, there for a moment, it looked to me like my Romeo was going to cry. His eyes were again so, so blue. It was as if Randall was looking right through my eyes and into the deepest depth of my love filled heart and soul!

Jesus had led me to this place in my life and now GOD was completing my soul with giving me a soul mate! Praise the Living GOD, for He is knows our hearts!

Within what seemed to be stilled moments, Randall took the small square, white box from his coat pocket, opened it and went down on one knee, caressing my hands in his hands. The noise of the passing cars were completely zoned out and all that I heard was Randall's sweet words, "Elizabeth, I love you with ALL my heart! I have never, ever loved any woman, like I love you at this very moment! When I get up in the morning, I think of you. When I'm at work, I wonder what you are doing. When I eat a meal, I wonder what you are eating. And when I go to bed, I pray that someday GOD will bring us together to be as "one" in my bed. With GOD as my witness, will you marry me and be my bride and my best friend?"

With Randall's proposal gently soaking into my ears, heart, and mind, I lowered my body down onto my knees, with my eyes riveted deeply into Randall's centre of concentration. I knew beyond a doubt that "Mr. Right" was found and now, again I was touched by his gentle guppy love and realized that this moment was the beginning of something very beautiful within our lives. Thank you Randall...Thank you, Jesus.

The words formed, tumbling out of my mouth, with zeal and excitement!

"Yes! Yes! Yes! I will be your wife, your best friend and your partner!" "I love you, Randall! And I have loved you for a long time now!

And with that he took the small engagement ring out of the box, lifted my hand and placed our commitment symbol tightly on my left hand, wedding ring finger. With the love band on my finger, we again embraced each other while down on our knees, while silently tears of joy streamed down my face. Together, Jesus, Randall and I were going to be a team and a Great team at that!

Only four years earlier, I had almost given up the Ghost. My body was at death's door, but when there had been no one to help me, Jesus stepped in and gave me breath in my body. Jesus saved my body, mind and soul from destruction and now the same Jesus was giving me a Christian life partner and a marriage made of Heaven, here on earth! Glory is to my Heavenly Counsellor, Physician and Love Author!

After a few long affectionate embraces and kisses, we dried our eyes, collected our selves, and headed once more back to our vehicle to go home. This again was a very large turning point in our lives. Randall, once single for five years after his first marriage divorce and I single for about a year and a half, had just invested our love into something way bigger than ourselves, and we both knew it.

Chapter Twelve
Wedding Bells

January 2, 1991 was here! Excitement was in the air! Our engagement commitment was coming to an end and by Wednesday 2:00 p.m., mountain standard time, I was starting my new life of marriage by exchanging vows with the man of my dreams!

All had gone well for the last four months of 1990, with school, Randall's and my children, our love relationship and also our housing. The fall of 1990 seemed to fly by once the new school year commenced once again and very soon, December was upon us!

The last week of December was a week off of school for us and we had set our wedding date for the middle of this week so that Randall and I could actually have a short, three day, winter honeymoon.

I ended the first half of the school year with one last name and started the second half of the school year, in 1991 with a brand new surname! How incredible is that!

Wednesday, January 2, 1991 was here! I awoke with a joyful song in my heart! I could hardly contain the notes inside my head! I was at my mother's apartment in downtown Medicine Hat and as I looked outside from the tenth floor, all I could see was that our wedding day had ice crystals in the frosty air. The atmosphere was calm with no wind, with only bright light snow crystals throughout the wintertime sky.

Our three boys looked so handsome in their white shirts, black pants and burgundy ties. We were, so proud of our children as they represented us, as part of our wedding party. Randall's beautiful young daughter graced us in pretty pink as she walked down the middle of the church with one of Randall's six brothers.

The Lutheran Church was all decorated with beautiful flowers and pink and white bows on the pews. The stained glass windows shone rainbows of glimmering, streaming colors.

As I stood behind the church door entrance looking into the Cathedral, my knees were weak. My heart was fluttering because at the Church Alter, my handsome, true love, Romeo was patiently waiting for me.

I was so nervous! Yet, I knew beyond a doubt that I was definitely doing the right thing! Never before had I experienced such an intimate, strong love. And yes, at this point of our relationship, I had no idea what limits my new husband would reach for me! I at that time, did not even have a clue as to what my dear husband to be, would sacrifice for my heart's true love, little me.

As the music cue for me to follow the precession down the aisle began, my eyes took in all our friends and family present with us on our special day. As I approached the front of the church, my total focus was "Randall". He was tall. He was a strong build with broad shoulders. He was unbelievably handsome! His piercing blue eyes warmed my soul as I was riveted to his total being. And yet, his face had a soft, gentle, caring smile, that once I reached the front of the pews, whispered softly, "Elizabeth".

By giving my life and soul to Jesus, I now was the recipient of a golden, hearted, Christian warrior! Praise GOD for GOD rewards those that seek HIM!

I, so far in my young life, had never been to a wintertime wedding and now I was experiencing first-hand the magic of such beauty at my own wedding! GOD truly was present and everything glistened!

The day unfolded without a hitch. Everything went perfectly! My dress that I had bought four months earlier, actually still fit and our four young children seemed to like each other and actually got along together.

With the wedding over and reception over, I could hardly wait to take off my wedding gear, dawn my honeymoon outfit and get into my little 1988 Dodge Sundance. We were heading for Lethbridge late in the afternoon and with great expectations, my emotional desires for my handsome groom, were growing!

With our suitcases intact in the trunk of the car, we giggled, chatted incisively, and told each other how much we loved each other. We could hardly keep our hands to ourselves! Our relationship for the last four months had been only partly physical and now with marriage papers and the blessings of Jesus, we were a bit, hot to trot.

We were driving into Taber, when I could stand it NO LONGER. I excitedly looked at my new, adorable husband and said: "Honey, do we have to travel all the way to Lethbridge tonight"? He smiled a sheepish smile, looking over at me and agreed: "Well"? "Not really".

It was settled! We took the very next turn off of Highway # 3, into the little town of Taber and drove right into a quaint little Taber Motel parking lot. Randall parked the car, and said he'll be right back. Eager and anxious, I awaited his return.

Soon Randall was back in the car, this time with the precious key to our nights stay, room. It was really a very small motel and we didn't have to drive too far to park the car in front of our room, which was lucky room number 28.

The weather temperature outside was starting to drop, but still the air was only beautiful ice crystals. It was like something out of a movie in a winter wonderland setting. Randall found the extension cord and plug in, plugged the car in and we carried our luggage into the small, cute motel room.

Now yes, we were on the anxious side of romance but we thought it to be, a good idea, to find a restaurant first, then, afterwards... sleep. Close by, as we ventured down the side road from our motel, we came across a small town, Chinese Food restaurant, went inside, ordered, ate and gaily made our way back for what turned out to be one of the busiest nights, that I can think of ever having.

Randall and I had never spent a whole evening and night together so far and what I experienced that sleepless night was truly worth waiting for!

My girlfriends, at an earlier wedding shower of mine, had bought some quite interesting paraphernalia, such as stick on, eatable tattoo's. Well, just before retiring to our queen size honeymoon bed, I retreated to the washroom to make ready for the romantic event. When I had changed into my night time clothes and tattoos, I hesitantly and awkwardly approached my newlywed husband.

We were both so eager for each other that, when we saw the other one, we instantly and tenderly embraced and kissed. As we started to shed our clothing, I don't know for sure what really happened but I started to giggle. The tattoos were sticky and some of them were starting to fall off. Randall, I don't think had ever seen such silly things before and so as he was trying to figure them out, he started to laugh also. They were sticking to him, to the bed sheets, some falling off and some sticking to me.

How amusing. There I was, Elizabeth, the sticky bride, laughing her head off while trying to make love to the man of her dreams. I looked like somewhat a bit of a clown minus the big red nose, which only made things worse. Tears of laughter, happiness and emotional release were streaming down our cheeks because Randall was also greatly amused with this relaxing and unwinding technique.

Finally after a good long laugh session, the dark night air was ours. Tenderness mixed with gentle caresses, were the starting of our unknown, yet GODLY future. Thank you Precious, Loving Lord Jesus for you are a giver of GOOD things! You are the author of "Love".

The night overflowed with two craving, love - filled hearts which now is history and somehow the morning was full of anticipation for wedding events yet to come. We loaded up our car with our suitcases, dusted off the fluffy white snow and were once again behind the wheel rolling into GOD's unknown future..., for us.

On that very special, January 2, 1991, wedding day of driving, it was the beginning of what has turned out to be, what seems to be a special winter weather driving blessing from Jesus. For every Christmas anniversary holiday between Boxing Day and January 2, Randall and I have had the privilege to travel short highway distances for two or three nights, to neighbouring cities, in the snow, to celebrate our wedding day. For the last 20 years, by the Grace of GOD, we have been able to travel by day, with brisk, bright sun-filled skies, to and from our winter holiday destinations. Only twice have we encountered winter flurries while driving and even then we were able to drive right out of the storm and into the calmness and crystal clearness of winter sunshine.

This might not seem to be a really big blessing to some, but for us in the middle of Alberta, Canada, great driving weather in the middle of Christmas time, IS a Big Blessing! And that's for 20 years of marriage now! Praise GOD!

In the beginning, as we were still two newly-weds, I was the recipient of a dream from the Lord. In the dream it was as though I was looking into a big square picture, and the square picture was of Randall and me, sitting in a car. With Randall in the driver's seat, and I in the passenger's seat, we started to drive, drive and drive. Up and down, all around, in and out and back up and down again.

It looked a bit like a roller-coaster track and we were the participants. It appeared to me that GOD was letting me know beforehand, that we were to do a lot of driving in our future. And by George, every Christmas holiday, we have driven hundreds of miles and the weather has mostly always been perfect!

Thank you, Jesus! Blessings come in ALL shapes and forms!

Chapter Thirteen
The Beginning of Traditions

On that very wonderful beginning of our romantic life encounter was also the start of a small yet meaningful tradition within our relationship.

Randall and I were, without a doubt, on a very frugal budget. Our get-a-way holidays and anniversaries were done on very little money. Most of the cost was gas, a motel room and yes, ladies, a little side trip to malls for some bargain hunting specials.

The gas, we weren't able to compromise on, but for the motel rooms, we shopped around until we found very moderately priced units. The best part was the shopping, which was always after Christmas Day and before New Year's Day, meant that everything was on sale!

We would come home after about 2 or 3 day's anniversary vacation, with treasures of all sort's. This included new clothing, item's for the house and also something bought for each other with a price limit of $5.00. Many times over the last 20 years, these small sentimental, sometimes purposeless gem's, were even engraved. We almost always wrote the anniversary year date on the bottom of our gifts and then, they were added faithfully to our collections.

At the malls, Randall and I would separate while going to search for that small meaningful item, to give to each other, while every year, trying lovingly to give something personal. This, for the first few years, wasn't a huge challenge, but as the years passed by, the challenge became more and more hard. Remember, our budget was set at $5.00 a gift. This was not the case because we were cheap, but because we just wanted to express our love in a non-monetary gesture. And sure enough, anniversary after anniversary, our gift hunt has always been successful.

Chapter Fourteen
Settling into New Family
Setting and Home

It was January 8ᵗʰ and the children and I were back in school. Randall was back at work and now it was time to settle into a major hectic routine! Our three day honeymoon had been perfect bliss in every way and now we had family reality take over.

Day in and day out, six lunches had to be prepared. The kids had to get up very early for school because we only had one bathroom. Most times in the morning, it seemed like we were imitating the army. Each person was only allowed 10 minutes in the bathroom for their stint. The bathroom timing was crucial therefore allowing time to dress, eat and make ready to get to school and work on time.

Therefore, many mornings in a regular timing zone, I found myself knocking or rather sometimes, pounding upon the bathroom door just firmly enough to hurry up the child inside. Anxiously, my voice and knocking, together simultaneously, roust-ed the awakening poor young soul to the attention of the moment.

GOD knows this part of our family arrangement was not easy and I apologise to all of our children for the inconvenience they experienced.

We had hockey practises, school events, home-work and more homework. It seemed that every daily moment was filled to the brim with something that HAD to be done. My housework many times, got left behind in my obligations.

Every school day, I had come home after my col-lege classes, made supper for six. We sat down and ate, took out the kids required homework, sat around the table and completed their papers and then I would start my homework, which was plenti-ful.

Many evenings the children could only play for an hour or so. The dishes had to be done, the kitch-en tidied and then it was their bedtime because our mornings came early. For literally two to three hours a night, after I had got the kids to bed, I would hit the pages of my texts.

GOD, help me! How was I going to manage this crazy schedule? However, as stressful as it was at times, I knew in my head and my heart that GOD would not give us more than we could handle. So day after day, week after week, we lived on a shoe string budget, worked as hard as we could muster, tried to be attentive to each child and our spouse, and reap the rewards of this timely, rambunctious, large blended family.

Even though money was scarce, Randall made plans for us as a family to go on vacations, at least minimally. For five years our busy, wholesome family encountered sibling challenges, work challenges, money challenges and just life challenges, but Randall and I always stuck together, with Randall always putting his faith in GOD first and then me. GOD was in every day of our lives and by GOD's Grace we intercepted each and every situation that life threw at us.

Thank you Precious Saviour for proving to us that Your Word is Truth.

Chapter Fifteen
The Old Green Rocket

Summer of 1991 was approaching. The kids were doing well. Our garage door had literally taken a beating by three ambitious boys. The white paint, now only covered bits and pieces of the nine foot square door and the dents were obvious.

However, our boys had settled into our hectic, meek and modest way of life without too much emotional friction. Thank GOD for happy children! And now that summer was here, Randall and I thought that maybe our little tribe could pack our old, small tent trailer with food, luggage, boys and us, attach it to our Old Green Rocket, meaning our old battered green1975 Ford Van and head for Banff, Alberta.

The kid's could sleep in the tent-trailer and Randall and I, could settle into the back of the van. Randall assured me that in the public camping areas, bears were not a factor to fear and the bottom line was, that this tent-trailer and van was all that we had or could afford.

It was, after a short family discussion, affirmative of all family members to schedule this summer vacation event! Banff it was going to be!

*   *   *

Summer was hot and the days were long and slow. Nothing was scheduled as we waited for the third and fourth week of July to come, while the kids played and were entertained by each other. Finally after two weeks of patiently waiting, 9:00 o'clock Monday morning came and our family vacation was here!

Suitcases packed, food packed, jackets packed and finally each one of us geared up and ready, we piled into the old green rocket. Randall made ready the tattered little tent-trailer, the night before our departure. Cleaned up, hooked up and piled up, we cheerfully shut up the van doors with everyone buckled in their seats' and we were off and running!

Chatting, giggling and playing games, everyone was right into the moment. The van had a round table, two captain chairs and a bench seat where the boys played cards, rolled dice and just enjoyed the excitement of the trip at hand.

The miles passed quickly, without much of a fuss. Calgary was approaching and all seemed to be under control, when...all of sudden a gruff, muffled noise starting coming from the underside of the van. Randall, the boys, and I listened, drove and listened. The noise seemed steady, kind of like the roaring of an ocean. As we continued up the high-way, Randall surmised that perhaps the muffler had a hole in it.

Wow, what next?

We got to Calgary and made our way through heavy traffic. All the while the hum of our vehicle just kept on humming. The boys were so good while they anticipated camping and the run of downtown Banff. Perhaps some chocolate fudge and perhaps a new ball cap would be the highlight of the day. Adventure, even with the van humming, was in the air.

After a school year of hard work and a year of settling into the Brady Bunch family, this vacation was truly a needed outlet of stress not only for the boys but also for us newlyweds.

The muffler mildly howled but we just kept on driving from the east side of Calgary, through Calgary to the west side. Ignoring the muffler, soon mountains were closing around us and Banff was just over the hill! The boys literally sat on the edge of their seats, buckled in, of course. Yes we had made it!! The scenery of green evergreens and green leafed trees were thick and beautiful! The van of course was loud and disappointing, but YES, we had made it and our little house abode was tailing nicely close behind us!

We turned left off of the main high-way and proceeded to make our way through downtown Banff with the trailer, loud old green van and a bundle of excited kids. We drove until we landed a parking stall large enough to hold our unit. Securely parked, we all tumbled out, counted heads, locked the doors and expectantly went looking for our adventures!

The boy's were only seven, nine and nine, so therefore Randall and I kept a close eye on them.

Store after store, intrigued us and drew us through their open swinging doors. We were among people from all nations, bustling along the sidewalk, chatting and visiting, also in search of precious treasures.

Jackpot! You could smell the chocolate fudge bars. This doorway certainly had something each one of us would love to spend our money on, that being our sweet tooth's. Each one of the boys seemed to be mesmerized by the smells and sights of these wonderful goodies and I knew such a purchase was exactly what we spent hours driving for.

Little brown bags in hand, of delicious treats melting in the hot weather and with permanent smiles glued onto our children's faces, we reluctantly exited the premises while yet still in search of even more surprises.

It seemed like we had only shopped for a short while, but actually the time blended one hour into hours, as we walked slower and slower. While searching out store after store, our feet and bodies became weary, hot and thirsty. Baseball hat's purchased, key chains, fridge magnets and a few other trivial items bought, we slowly but surely made our trek back to our welcoming, patiently waiting, old green van.

Night was coming and we still had to find a camping ground. Randall knew his way around Banff a bit and soon we were parked at a campground crest at a higher altitude. The campground wasn't too far from the Banff town site and was patrolled regularly by the park wardens.

Relieved and dead tired, Randall, the boys and I, set up camp. With a campfire made, jackets dawned for the evening and wiener sticks cooking us a bedtime meal of hotdogs and marshmallows, we soaked up the peace, the quiet, the beauty and the enjoyment of each one of us being there.

Randall always states that he finds GOD in the wilderness, outdoors amongst the evergreens and pure air. Well GOD was certainly with us as we talked, sang and just relaxed in GOD's great frontroom as the veil of darkness draped the sky with a large yellow, man in the moon and stars shining brilliantly down upon a very happy, exhausted yet content family.

The day's events had been full of adventure, full of driving, walking, eating, trinkets, surprises and now it was time to crawl under the covers in our modest outdoor camping bed's.

GOD is so good! With simply nothing but peace and joy in our hearts and full stomachs, we retired into our night time dreams and dreamed dreams of where only dreams can take us. Soon it would be morning and again, we would be on the road to adventure!

Thank you Jesus for the simple pleasures that permeate deep down into our souls, to feed us and fill us with love to the brim!

Chapter Sixteen
West Edmonton Mall, Here We Come

With still five days remaining of our family holiday, Banff was terrific and now our attention was drawn towards Edmonton's great attention getter, West Edmonton Mall! The muffler was still intact, a little louder every mile driven, but still intact. Randall checked on it every short stop we made. We were still safe.

Again, as we trekked northward, the boy's played table games, ate sandwiches, and entertained each other like boy's will do. Our family had never been to Edmonton before as a family, let alone this huge mall. Again the anticipation of what we may see, kept the excitement flowing between each one of us.

After what seemed like a long, long time of driving towards our destination, we were at the outskirts of this large centre. The muffler was on its last leg and the loud "hum" coming from under the vans carriage started to pierce our ears and drown out our indoor voices. However, it was Sunday and all the garages with mechanics, were closed.

Navigating van and trailer, Randall carefully followed my map and road instructions, leading us to our first night's stay, which was close to the West Edmonton Mall. After, unfortunately missing a couple of turns, we made our way back and hook or by crook, there in sight was a small motel which by golly had an outdoor swimming pool. This seemed wonderful to the boys, and the "great mall" was in birds eyes view also.

The motel had vacancies and we were tired, excited and dirty. Randall rented a room with two beds and a hide-a-bed pullout. Randall, the boy's and I could wash up and then enjoy a swim. It wasn't too long at all and all five of us were clean again and heading for the open swimming pool!

The sun was out shining brightly and the warm water felt warm and wonderful. After what seemed like a lot of horse play, water dunking and swim tag, our stomachs began to make growling noises!

Since evening was approaching quickly, our swimming fun came to a close much too soon. It was getting late and supper-time was starting to get close. When we finally had changed into some suitable clothing and headed out for a meal, it turned out to be a treat, because close by was a quaint little restaurant with pasta, burgers and other appetizing food entrees. On the home front, eating out was rare and when we did, it was mostly at Mac D's, so this was also a pleasure anticipated by all.

One thing is for sure: Growing boy's have good appetites! And with a long day of driving, so did Randall and I.

The next day, Monday morning, came bright and early. Again anticipation was in the air! Sights and sounds of West Edmonton Mall were soon to be ours! Breakfast finished at a moderate restaurant next door and again, three young boys, parents and a noisy muffler were off again in our old green van, Mr. Faithfull.

The mall wasn't too hard to find, give or take an extra driven block or two, but sure enough there it was, big and beautiful in all its glory. As we followed the signs, we soon found ourselves in a designated underground parking lot, which I might mention was almost totally full of parked vehicles of all different sizes and shapes.

As we drove around searching for an empty parking stall, we had to settle for a parking stall quite a distance from the mall's entrance. No big deal, we had made it!

With our money almost burning a hole in our pockets, we organized ourselves, locked the van up and made our way to the nearest entrance. When we got inside our eyes could hardly believe the sights and sounds of so many stores and attractions. It looked at first impressions that there really was something for every one of us. Jeans, tops and perhaps a belt for each one of our children were possibly in the buying picture, with maybe a special pair of runners to top each outfit off.

Our location established and watches synchronized, I can't believe it now, but we let the boys go as a three-some, to search out the stores they were interested in. Cell phones had not been invented yet. I suppose children were safer, way back then, but that independence we gave the boy's way back then, makes me shudder with fear as I think of it now. No way now on a hill of beans, would I now consider such poor judgement!

By the Mercy of GOD, the boys shopped, went on the Farris wheel and ride attractions, went swimming in the biggest wave pool I have ever seen and returned safe and sound after many hours spent within this historic monument, West Edmonton Mall. Randall and I tried to be close by, keeping our eyes on them from a close distance and meeting with them to take their bought goods out to our van. Thank you and praise our Living Saviour!

About two hours into our shopping trip, Randall decided to take a walk outside to the now quiet green van, to check out the under carriage, namely the muffler.

On returning to our family group, Randall had a very, now funny story to share. As the lighting in the parking lot was quite dim, the parking lot security gentleman was quite alarmed when, as he walked past our van, my dear husband was banging around under the van.

The banging was apparently quite loud and yes, I suppose, quite suspicious. The security guard was under the impression that an unknown, someone, namely Randall, was attempting to steal this van, because all the guard could see was a pair of runners attached to legs, sticking out from under this old poor green parked van.

Well, after Randall was made to come out from under the van, the security guard interrogated him verbally and also checked him for wallet ID. With driving credentials, picture ID and license in hand, the guard was finally satisfied and Randall was then able to resume his muffler fixing.

It wasn't too long thereafter and the muffler was wired onto the van body again, at least until we could see Doctor Muffler, somewhere close by. It was Monday and the garages were open again, thank goodness!

About six hours had passed and we were exhausted and broke. The boy's and us had a superb time! It really was as great as we had anticipated and now with all of us back in tow, we made our way back to our motel and swimming pool.

After dropping the clan off, Randall drove directly to the nearest garage station where our lose muffler got a complete overall in no time at all. Amazing! Big dollars and the next afternoon, we owned still an old green van, but the muffler purred like a kitten.

Our Edmonton visit was spent rather quickly with all sorts of travels within Edmonton and soon it was time to head for Medicine Hat once more. On the way home we hit Calgary Zoo and a Calgary water park. The van ran well, we all had a great time away from home and by the end of the second week we were definitely ready to sleep in our own beds.

That vacation was truly one of the best family holiday's that we had enjoyed in our young blended family life!

Chapter Seventeen
Dad's Reassuring Kiss

S hortly after Randall and I tied our marriage knot, I was to be the recipient of a very special "kiss."

As GOD is a GOD of wonderful surprises, when we least expect it, the hand of our Heavenly Father is upon us!

When Randall and I purchased our first home, our family consisted of three young boys, a daughter and us two adults, which meant that we needed a five bedroom house. Now that in its self was a tough goal to reach because, again, we didn't have much money income.

I had $5,000.00 and Randall had $5,000.00, for each of us to put into a home for the down payment. By the Grace of GOD, we did find a house with three bedrooms on the main floor and two bedrooms in the basement, within our price range. Thank you, GOD for answering prayers!

It was about the middle of March, right around my birthday and about three months after our wedding date. All our family was tucked in bed for a night of rest when very early in the a.m., as the dawn was quickly approaching and Randall and I were fast asleep, I was awakened with a loving kiss on my cheek.

The "kiss" was very distinct, loving and gentle. I immediately awoke and sat up in bed. Looking all around and down at Randall, I saw that Randall was fast asleep and there was no one else in the room with Randall and I. It had just turned 4:15. Somehow in my spirit I knew beyond a doubt that my deceased dad, who on his death bed had asked Jesus for forgiveness and also had asked Jesus into his heart, had returned in spirit, to give me his blessings. He was giving approval of Randall and our marriage union, with a sealing kiss. I felt deep down in my own spirit that the man I had chosen for my new husband was also the preferred choice of my deceased father.

This "feeling" or "spiritual knowledge" was strong and definite.

As I laid my head back down on my pillow, I silently thanked my dad for his approval and then, my Lord, for I knew also that my "Jesus" was in charge of every aspect of my being. Thank you, precious Jesus, for saving my father from eternal "Hell" and giving my dad, life forever.

Since that spiritual encounter with my maternal father, twenty years ago, early that spring morning I have not experienced any further spiritually awakening encounters with him of any kind. I believe his assignment for me is finished and that he is now enjoying the green hills of the "Heavenly" city and one day, sometime in the future, we shall meet again.

Chapter Eighteen
Amazing! I Can See!

One thing I've seemed to learn first-hand by my life experiences is that, we are what we think we are, and also, sometimes we make funny mistakes. I am no exception to that rule of thumb.

Since I've been eight years old, I have had to wear very thick eye glasses. At six years old, I would watch television, and not even realize what I was not seeing. First grade was taught to me in a grey fog-like atmosphere. I didn't realize it, and neither did the teacher, but I only understood about half of the teachings because my eyes were so poor. My ears had to work overtime so my stress levels increased and my personal self esteem plunged.

In grade twelve of my schooling, I had a wonderful opportunity to change my big heavy eye glasses in for a pair of "hard" prescribed contact lenses. The maintenance of, the such, was quite involved but I jumped at this beautiful eye glass freedom opportunity the moment my eyes were considered mature enough for the lenses, by my optometrist.

For the first time in my life I had a licence to see and see well without covering up my face with a heavy frame and even heavier lenses. Back then the lenses were made from cut glass, not plastic, hence, "coke bottle bottom glasses."

Sixteen years after Randall and I married, I was still wearing my contact lenses full time. I wore them for 12 hours a day, at least, and seven days a week.

About four months after Randall and I were married, I had a very funny event happen to me. Since GOD had been very active in my new life, I was very focused on the Goodness of GOD and possible miracles He was doing for me.

It was a normal night of sleep and morning came quietly as usual. But as I opened my eyes to begin the day, I rolled over, picked up my alarm clock, looked at the numbers and immediately was amazed how well I could see! With great excitement I immediately looked all around... I could see!! How could that be?!! Hallelujah!! I can't see hardly anything without my glasses on! But now, I could see!! Since Jesus had done so, so many miracles in my life since I became a born again Christian only a few years earlier, I just automatically assumed that, by the Grace of GOD, Jesus had healed my eyes!

I jumped up and out of our bed and then it happened. My eye sockets were starting to stick with dryness. Then my eyes started to blur from the stickiness.

I knew, within seconds of this eye reaction that, da, my contact lenses were still on my eye balls from the day before! I couldn't believe how dumb I had been to forget to take the lenses out at bedtime the night before. Looking and feeling very sheepish at my extreme forgetfulness and then rupturing excitement, I made my way to the washroom, took out the crispy dry disks, washed my dry, red eyes and face and then proceeded to wake up the rest of my quietly, sleeping family members.

It took many years before I shared my humiliation miracle with any of my friends, but when I do, everyone listening, has a great laugh over it, and, so do I. Maybe someday Jesus WILL heal my eyes, but for now I'm back in stylish eye wear glasses and it's not all that bad.

I do believe that GOD has a sense of humour because on that early morning sitting on the side of my bed, I looked and acted quite like a clown, only I didn't know I looked like a clown until GOD brought me back to reality. I know Jesus is with me always, because His word states in His GOOD BOOK that He will never leave us nor forsake us. GOD is all Truth and Sovereign, therefore He cannot lie and that is all I need to know. Thank you, Jesus.

Chapter Nineteen
Work and Love Making

Very early in our marriage, which actually was our wedding night in that little town motel, I learned that my husband was really an idealistic romantic. Randall always pursued me with loving words. He was always pouring uplifting words of encouragement into my ears and soul. He was in essence, rebuilding my broken down ravaged self-esteem from my previously ill-torn life.

After the first three months of dating Randall, I knew he was a caring loving sincere gentleman. I thought on our wedding day that I knew him pretty well and that I loved him with all of my heart, but as the years unfolded, I realized later, that on that wonderful wedding day, the meaning of true love, was only starting for us.

It wasn't long into our married life that I realized, as Randall was wowing me with verbal and physical romance, that his zeal to accomplish regular yard, household, vehicle and any other type of work related duties seemed to be spurred on after I gave myself to him in the close fines of our bedroom.

The more I allowed Randall to nourish my mind, body and soul with the only genuine love form he knew, the more, day by day my soul started to heal from all the previous heart ache and pain.

Over and over again, there seemed to be a pattern forming. Soon, I realized the love making was somehow attached to getting chores done also. Randall was always extremely energized after love making and wanted always to please me more by accomplishing the most menial or the biggest task that needed to be done around our house and busy life schedule.

Grass was cut, trees were pruned, lunches sometimes were made, but family moral was always lifted when the love between us was shown to each other in the privacy of our bedroom.

GOD's Holy Book claims that GOD is Love. Well only two years earlier, broken and tormented, I had sat in my car late one night, turned to the empty passenger seat and talked to Jesus as if he was right there in the empty seat beside me. On that occasion is when I asked, in tears, for Jesus to give me a man to love me and share my life. For Jesus to give me a man that would love me for what was in my heart.

Plus I asked Jesus to give me a man that would love me no matter of my status in life. I also asked Jesus to give me a man that would walk beside me as my best friend and hold me when I needed a hug. To have a man that would love my children and help me raise them from young children to adulthood. A man with GODLY morals who had Jesus at the center of his heart, just like my heart, because then I knew I could trust him.

GOD only knows that what I was asking Jesus for was, through me, almost impossible. But GOD's Word also says that, "With GOD all things are possible" and when we ask GOD for anything from our hearts desires, GOD always gives an answer back if we just believe and trust Him.

Well as GOD would have it, GOD answered my plea and then only five or six months later, Randall came into my budding rebuilding life and I received all the ingredients of characteristics that my heart's desires, had been so much hungry for.

I fell in love with Randall for his gentleness, his wisdom and undying caring love for me and all our children. I love him so much for showing me daily his mission of love towards me! I adore his actions of sincere love words and physical caresses brought to me through the arms of GOD's ambassador, Randall, my precious groom.

And yes, I never knew how romance and work could be related, but yes, a lot of inside and outside chores have been accomplished daily by my very personal champion spouse. By the Grace of GOD, I have become a "Bride Princess" and I truly am eternally grateful!

Thank you GOD for unconditional LOVE!

Chapter Twenty
My Mother and Randall's Strong Arms

Along with marrying, me, and taking under his wings of responsibilities, our four young children, Randall also adored my mother. My mother, Agnes, truly was my example of courage and strength in life, therefore a dear "Hero" formed in my heart and mind. My mother of sixty some years old, had been stricken with MS at the young age of 34 years old and now she had a son-in-law that respected and loved her and our family.

The first time I took Randall to my mother's high-rise apartment for a supper meal and to spend the evening with Mom and my Grandmother, I eagerly watched the evening unfold and awaited to hear my mother's opinion of the new gentleman in my life.

The evening went smoothly, with lots of caring chatter. I helped Mom with the meal, as my Mother was wheelchair bound yet very independent and capable with living on her own. My Grandmother was full of laughter and appreciation on meeting this fine young man, who, in my Grandmothers words, was a fine, gentle, caring man.

My Grandmother was a short, plump, 80ish, very, convicted faithful Christian prayer warrior and her approval of Randall was indeed respected and sought.

My dear Mother had always been quiet and passive. She went about her business as a doer not a busybody but when she did comment, you knew it was a carefully thought out statement or opinion. Mom lived by her motto that if she had nothing good to say about someone, well then, she would say nothing!

Supper dishes washed and visiting over with, the evening came to a close. Full satisfied stomachs, coffee and interesting conversations were the result of our first supper meal together, with my new found prince, Randall and the most important women in my life.

I could barely wait for the next day, to hear my Mother's and Grandmother's observation comments of this member of the opposite sex, so... quite early the next morning, I was on the phone, inquiring.

The only thing my Mother stated was that Randall's eyes never left my positioning within the apartment. Mom noted that as I moved within the kitchen preparing supper, Randall's eyes focused patiently and lovingly upon me, watching my every move!

I had no idea that he was so intrigued with what I do or how I do it!

My Grandmother and Randall had encountered quite a conversation including Christian faith within his family and our family. Through their conversation, my Grandmother's heart was won over just like mine!

Jesus is So GOOD! Again my Saviour was answering prayer, right before my eyes!

My new love and romantic partner was a hit right from the beginning. Such a gem, I had no idea was possible!

A year and a half later and six months into our new marriage, we lived in a modest five bedroom bungalow, with three small bedrooms on the main floor and two bedrooms in the basement of our home. It was our first summer together as a blended family and we decided to invite Mom and Grandma over to our house for an afternoon of visiting.

Well, my Mother had never been lifted and carried out of the car she arrived in, ever before. Normally, I would help her to slide out of the car and into her wheelchair. We had managed many outings, shopping trips, dining out events, and visiting places, by car using the means of wheelchair transportation, in and out of the car.

But now, my beloved groom, decided upon himself to transport my Mother directly from the vehicle into our home, via the back door, within the clutch of his strong arms. I had no idea that my Mother was so intensely nervous of completing this feat! I knew that we would not be able to manoeuvre her wheelchair through the back door and up the three steps into the kitchen, so I too thought that carrying her really was a great idea.

Once she was out of the car and squarely picked up and nestled onto Randall's chest and arms, the fun was about to unfold. Making their way up the driveway, up the back sidewalk and in through the outside back door, all seemed to be going well. That is until Randall, with Mom, tried to make the assent up the inside back three steps and through the kitchen doorframe.

Stepping up onto the third step and onto the main floor, Randall seemed to get stuck! How could he be stuck?!! He backed down a step and tried to enter the kitchen again, only this time with more force. What was going on?!

The second time, he stepped down and back, gently yet very focused on keeping Mom upright in a sitting position. His arms felt like they were being torn from his body! His strength was beginning to ebb! Mom was tall but not overweight, yet she was starting to feel a bit like a dead weight, hundred and some pound bag of potatoes.

Watching from behind, I had no idea what the problem was at hand. I just stood there witnessing my husband's great useless effort and my mother hanging from his arms, silently, yet proactive.

On Randall's fourth try of entry, with much deliberate force, and a loud sort of "growl" that came from the very depth of his being, he successfully bulldozed through the open doorway. As the two of them were now on the inside of the kitchen, Randall proceeded to settle Mom into her wheelchair. With great relief, Randall said to Mom, "What was that"?! "What was stopping us from getting inside"?!

That's when Mom smiled meekly and replied, "I was scared so I hung onto the doorframe."

For a weak, elderly, MS stricken, woman, Randall could not believe the strength and resistance he had just encountered! After a couple of days had passed the "proof was in the pudding" as to say, as my determined Mother was the recipient of big black and blue bruises on both of her upper arms.

She almost took a strapping, strong young man to his knees and he didn't even know she was doing it! Now that's determination!!

Love you, Mom, and always will. You're my "Hero".

Like I have said before, my Mother was a gentle, soft spoken, kind, generous woman. On very few and far between occasions did I ever hear my mother comment a negative statement about another person, dead or alive. But one thing that was so funny, that it was actually quite cute about my mother, was her comment to me on one of her visits, while at our home.

On her return to the kitchen from our washroom, Mom politely, yet matter of fact like, told me that I had the toilet paper on the roll "backwards!!" Yup, I said "backwards!"!

As I was whipping the potatoes, I could hardly believe the conviction in her soft voice. I didn't want to hurt Mom's feelings, but this sounded so silly to me that a controlled smile crossed my face. I did realize however, that she was dead serious and somehow, she needed to tell me about this problem.

GOD, Bless her sweet heart but, GOD forgive me, no I didn't go and fix the looming problem!

Isn't it funny, the smallest things we remember of our loved ones, many years later, when we look back? Our Mother's may be gone for many, many years, but deep down in the depth of our hearts core, when we take the time to sit quietly and remember them, their very spirits come to our hearts surface, dancing vividly in our minds memories.

And if your Mother is still alive, sharing life experiences with you, give her some of your precious, busy time. Cherish her, forgive her, but mostly accept her and love her. For many years earlier, she looked after you the best she was able. Now the roles may be reversed and she may need you, her child, to be her advocate.

Honour your mother and father the best you can, for this is one of GOD's Ten Commandments and GOD say's he WILL bless you more abundantly when you obey HIS WORD.

Chapter Twenty-One
Puck in the Wagon

Those first five years in our first home was indeed full of surprises, not only for us but also our children.

Over the five year period of time, with three growing hockey nut boys, our garage door was dented, scraped and abused seriously. White tattered paint hung loosely from huge bits and pieces of raw metal, indented like a cake mould in a foreign design. By the time we moved to another home, the garage door had taken a beating like I've never seen before because it seemed the boy's hockey net just wasn't big enough!

As the boy's played street hockey on our driveway for hours on end, many times, Randall would take them on, yielding a hockey stick of his own.

Randall loved to play hockey during winter months just like our son's and I think he wanted to "shine" also in the hockey arena, after all, our grown men, husbands, really are "boy's" at heart.

It seemed that hockey and pucks were played in our side yard driveway! Hockey and pucks were in our back yard! Even our unfinished basement, the boy's wielded hockey sticks and rubber pucks! Randall, playfully always seemed to gravitate towards playing a little bit of hockey with our boy's, which I know the boy's also enjoyed. It warmed my heart to see the bonds of love grow between our children and Randall, that being Randall's son and my boy's new stepdad.

It was on one of these fun occasions that we were in for a "surprise," like where the puck would land.

Randall, the kid's and I were outside enjoying the summer air in our backyard while the boy's were doing their regular hockey stuff. Randall, all of a sudden, stepped up to the plate, so to speak, to challenge our son's, as to who could land the rubber puck into the net, which was placed close to the back fence.

We were standing quite a ways away from the net, close by the back of the house. Our fence was about six feet high and we were about seventy-five feet from the front of the orange and white net target.

Being the Dad, Randall let the boy's aim and fire the puck towards the net first, youngest to oldest. Then in all his splendour, it was Dad's turn. With all our eye's on the man of the house, what happened next, we could hardly fathom. We certainly DID NOT see this coming!

All eyes, on Randall with hockey stick in hand and hard black puck on grass at his feet, there was deep, thoughtful aim and finally, with great effort, a strong, forceful swing! With a look of forced determination on Randall's face, his eyes and all of our eyes were glued to the little black puck in question.

With great speed, the flying disk flew quickly and quietly through mid air, landing squarely in the middle of our back alley neighbours station wagon car. The misplaced puck flew up, up and past the six foot fence, straight, with enormous impact through the side back window of the restaurant owner's vehicle.

This station wagon had un-expectantly become the new "net."

All our eye's bulged from surprise and horror! Especially Randall's eyes! His expression was totally priceless!

As fast as the puck landed and shattered the glass, Randall was hightailing his way towards the accident site, while the boy's and I trailed closely behind, still in complete disbelief.

On viewing the broken glass at a closer bird's eye view, Randall instructed us to all go back in our back yard while he went inside the restaurant and in-formed the car owner of the predicament of his mangled car.

The end of this tiny mishap wasn't too serious since Randall was a licensed Auto Body Mechanic, and it was in his power to pay for and fix the broken window. The car owner was put at ease. All ended well and that was the last fireball hockey puck, Randall, aimed so loosely towards the small net in front of a six foot fence while we lived in that house! Praise God!

Now as we and our grown children look back at that incident, we have to chuckle because, funny how our playful young boys were always busy in the yard, it wasn't them that got into trouble, it was dear dad. Bless his heart!

Chapter Twenty-Two
Little Mitzy

The years were unfolding and the home front had changed some. Our children were growing older and some of them had decided to live with their other parents. Our home was emptier of people but evidently was full of GOD's presence.

In August of 1996 I had taken on the position of Nanny/Housekeeper for a husband and wife teacher team couple and my mornings always started at 6:00 a.m. I was always up, dressed and readied to leave the house by 6:30 a.m. and I would return home from work close to 5:30 p.m. Needless to say with putting in eleven hours away from home, Monday to Friday, I was ready for a nap after supper many evenings.

We had a little black and white, pushed in nose, Boston Terrier that was a sweet addition to our home. We had adopted her from the animal shelter and her name was Mitzy. We adopted Mitzy when our children were still living with us. We watched Mitzy thrive as she played with our young children.

We always thought Mitzy was extremely talented, just like our own kids because, no where before had we seen a dog jump into her own bed and proceed to cover herself up with her own quilt. First Mitzy would nudge her pushed in nose under one side of the quilt, pushing with her little body, making a tossing motion with her neck and finally pulling an edge of the quilt with her sharp teeth until she was completely covered from head to tail under the blanket, snug as a bug in a rug!

For many years, on our arrival of coming home from our jobs and school, we each were greeted with a wagging tail stub, licks, drool and excitement! If I was at home waiting for Randall to arrive from work, there at the top of the steps was Mitzy, patiently sitting, waiting and waiting for Randall's timely welcome home. Mitzy truly was a blessing from GOD for each one of us, for she was unconditional open heart loving, no matter what time of day it was.

Unfortunately our daughter and two sons moved out, leaving our family down to our second oldest son, Jeffery, Randall my husband and me, Elizabeth. My work day's increased to eleven hour days and our sweet loving puppy was left deserted for hours on end. GOD, please forgive us for this tragedy within our home!

Our own little cheering section, Mitzy, was destined to hours on end of loneliness and eventually, a broken heart.

After about a year of our long working days by herself, Mitzy stopped greeting us at the entrance of our home. Her tail stopped wagging, her barks of welcome abated. Her licks and drool were kept from us. She was dying with a broken heart of loneliness.

Randall and I felt deeply guilty of such an offense to such a beautiful family member, but GOD knew that we HAD to work. We had no choice! We had to give our puppy away, hopefully to a loving household with children, like we had years earlier. Maybe we could save her life by giving back to her a, life of living.

So one day we said a little prayer and then put an advertisement in the newspaper under the "Free" section, hoping for a new family for our dear little dog.

Well it wasn't even a full week and our prayers and advertisements were answered. A young couple with two small children called us, beaming with great enthusiasm wanting to share their family home with our caring loving Boston Terrier. Praise GOD! GOD knew and so did we that it was time to let Mitzy go. She needed freedom from our emptied home so that she could thrive once again in a child and parents, full home!

Chapter Twenty-Three
Angel Awareness

It was around the same year that we owned Mitzy, that Randall saw one of my angels, sitting quietly on the edge of my bed while I was fast asleep.

I had been working nine hour days, getting up at 6:00 a.m., leaving our home at 6:30 a.m. and arriving back home for the evening and supper at 5:30 p.m. This schedule was a Monday to Friday work routine that went on for two years.

By Friday evenings my body's energy was mostly spent. Therefore, after making supper, many times I would lie down for up to an hour, stealing a time of much needed sleep, before my regular bedtime, at 10:00 p.m.

I never knew it until later on, but Randall would check in on me to make sure I was tucked in nicely under the covers, during that hour. Having this short, needed sleep allowed me to always be able to get up very early again each weekday morning.

Well, one evening I crawled into my bed again for a nap, as usual, but this evening something would be a bit different. On awakening and coming back into the living-room to be with my loving husband everything seemed normal, but there was one amazing thing different! Soon in conversation with Randall, I was informed that Randall had peeked into our bedroom, again as usual, to check on me.

However, this time, when Randall's eyes focused in the dimly lit room, there beside me, sitting sideways, with her feet touching the floor, was the figure of a slim female, in a white gown. He described her as having long, straight, blond hair and as soon as his eyes focused on her being there, she disappeared.

This vision of my angel was truly only for a moments second, but Randall knew after seeing her, exactly how her appearance was. Randall knew instantly that he had seen an angel watching over me as I slept! Praise GOD!

I was also amazed, but also very comforted by Randall's relayed information to me about her, because I believe everyone has at least one guardian angel.

We are not called to pray to angels, but rather to pray to The Holy Trinity, for GOD to send His angels to protect us in times of danger. Now I know that when we do ask, HE answers by sending.

Now after twenty five years since asking Jesus into my heart, GOD has made it possible for me to meet my guardian angel during a dream, while sleeping and the angel Randall saw beside me on my bed. Both of these angelic Beings were dressed in a white long gown. The angel in my dream, however, was very distinct because of the huge white wings that empowered her whole, beautiful, strong essence!

My eyes were totally focused on the immense, stretched out; powerful wingspan of her incredible white wings on her body, yet the gentle, loving look of a caregiver sent by GOD Himself, for my protection.

Her mouth never moved, but with a still soft voice, she spoke to me saying, "I have been with you from the beginning." And I knew beyond a doubt that "yes" this strong, beautiful angelic creature had been assigned to me from GOD from before the time I was in my mother's womb.

Thank you, Jesus, for this moment and Word of Truth.

Chapter Twenty-Four
As the Years Keep Unfolding

As time has a way of keeping on ticking, Randall and I continued to live, laugh, love and enjoy each other. Our children were getting older and our love for each other was getting cemented deeply into each other's hearts. But even a solid 8 in love has its limits!

My dear caring husband decided early on in our marriage that he and a friend would attempt an annual autumn fishing trip in the mountains and I would stay home and hold the fort down and take care of the kid-lets. This seemed to be acceptable to me because I wanted Randall to have a hobby to do, like fishing that he really enjoyed and could look forward to every year.

Summer soon was over and the autumn week of a boating and fishing adventure was right around the corner. Our tent trailer was packed. The boat and motor was readied. Warm clothing were washed and packed also. The hour of departure was closing in and I thought everything would go smoothly? Ha!

September 7, 1993 my husband and his friend, in their two trucks pulling a tent trailer with one truck and a boat with the other, finally said there farewells and voila, a week of being a bacheloress began! Our Indian summer was here. The temperature was above zero. The trees were glistening with a beautiful yellow, gold and red and the wind was still.

Our children were settled into another year of schooling and I was in between my last office job and working at a large, local grocery store.

The first couple of days without Randall seemed to pass uneventful, but by the third day somehow, three missing plastic wall tiles that were surrounded by three walls of unblemished tiles, got my attention. Somehow by the fourth day I just could not stand the three missing, three square inch plastic wall tiles. GOD forbids such a sight!

Please don't ask me what I was thinking! Only GOD knows for sure why I started to yank and tear every good three inch plastic wall tile from its glued in secure place! The more I yanked the perfect squares from the wall the better I felt. The kids were in school and I was in some kind of daytime nightmare! It didn't take too long at all and I had stripped naked the three walls! Then, unfortunately, it looked a bit like the carcass of a big bird without feathers! Then when only the unsightly yellow glue marks remained, the telephone rang, just like right on cue and amazing enough it was the "Gone Fishing" man of the house, Randall.

Was I to share with him the "Bathroom" news now or wait for his arrival home? I really did NOT want to ruin the rest of Randall's little holiday get away, so...my lips were sealed...at least for now!

Our telephone conversation was brief and full of missing each other, tender love cues and verbal gestures but with great wisdom, my bathroom mission accomplished was unspoken of.

The next couple of days flew by quickly and with great excitement the kids and I were expecting Randall's arrival home. I was about to witness great compassion, like I had never seen before from any man, towards me, even when my actions were very disturbing.

Randall was home! He walked in, dirty and smelling like fish, sweat, and B.O, but he was home again safe and sound! Praise GOD, the man I gave my heart to, was home again!

I had never, ever been alone in my bed and house for a whole week while married before, so my sweet foul smelling husband really was a wonderful sight for sore eyes! His clothes and body were reeking, but his ear to ear smiling lips and deep radiant blue eyes sparkled brightly, piercing my heart with his genuine love for me. He truly missed me and was absorbed in the moment of seeing me again.

After, a lips only touching welcome, we started to exchange our past weeks news, which then led both of us to my construction site, our main and only house bathroom.

Our conversation went something like this: "Elizabeth, you look beautiful as always! How was your week at home with the kids? I've missed you Sooo much honey"!

I knew I couldn't deny what I had done to our home's bathroom and it was NOT pretty! The only way I could explain myself to my groom was to sheepishly say "I love you honey...Please don't be mad...I'll help to fix it! Honestly, I couldn't help myself"!

And then I took him to the bathroom...

The walls seemed to screech at top volume, "FIX ME"!

Randall's eyes fixated on the bare glued surface of the walls! His mouth dropped to his chin! Panic was written all over his ridged body and stone face. All he could do was quietly murmur, "No...NO...NO Way...This can't be real"?

But like a mute, I stood there just waiting for the reality of the bare walls to soak in and a couple of moments later, it did.

When the initial shock released my husband's body from statue form, all heck broke loose and I became the witness of a mighty worrier in great dance mode. Randall's arms and legs were flying! He looked like he was the Chief of a great rain dance in the middle of a vast dessert. His mouth was spitting out all kinds of concerns plus a few profanities while

I silently took a few steps backwards, out of the line of fire!

"Oh, GOD please help me...and PLEASE calm my sweet husband".

The whole time of Randall's reaction, all I could think to myself was, "GOD, PLEASE let Randall FORGIVE ME"! That's all I could think, because I loved my husband with all of my heart and no way possible did I want to tear his life apart. He was such a conscientious, caring man and father. I loved him so much and I didn't want to see him in emotional pain.

A few minutes passed of his body language and verbal eruption and then...dead silence!

Within minutes the ranting and raving abated and my Randall cooled down.

Believe me, he wasn't very happy about the bathroom walls, but his love for me was stronger than the offence I had committed. GOD was answering my prayers. Randall was still ticked at me but somehow deep inside of him, his love for me was accepting my construction efforts and stupidity. Now that is "Love".

In the very early stages of our life together, on the tail end of Randall's first annual fishing getaway, I learned a very big lesson and received amazing compassion from the only man that has ever really loved me, for me. I learned what unconditional love really is, and now, I hope with prayer, that I will be able to give back, to my loving husband, the same, throughout our unfolding years of matrimony.

Jesus is "GOOD" and teaches us many values through our loved ones He sends into our lives. Thank you, Lord, for many beautiful blessings, for your compassion and love are real.

And yes, our tattered bathroom walls were repaired, but this time not with plastic tiles. The man of the house, well, did a great job! Thank you, Lord, for mercy, compassion and true love.

Chapter Twenty-Five
Flamboyant Kitchen Cupboards

In the early years of our married life, as our lives seemed to be over the top busy with four kids, school, work and sports, it seemed also that I loved to decorate our modest bungalow home. The furniture, wall pictures and scattered room ornaments were mostly from second hand stores but all were gathered with dignity, "Love" and dreams of having a beautiful environment. For literally most of our twenty year marriage, never did "second hand" furniture and decor bother either Randall or me. Randall was just so happy that I was content and happy!

As I also was growing in self confidence and self awareness of being loved, I was about to test my prince charming's love for me again, but didn't realize it until "after" the fact!

I had been out of work for a couple of months when it all started. I received a lump sum of pay from my unemployment insurance government check. The money had been held up for a couple of months and our family had been living off of Randall's wages, which was an experience all in itself. Summer had arrived and now so had almost a thousand dollars, Praise GOD!

As I looked at the multiple mini checks in my hands, I gleamed and almost immediately knew what I wanted to do with them. Our kitchen floor squeaked badly with every step taken and the visual condition of our flooring was tattered, old and poor. There previously had been no way possible to repair and update our homes kitchen, that is, until now! This was like found money that had not been earmarked for anything in particular! Again, a special thank you to Jesus was in order!

Randall knew a lot of men in the construction field and happened to know someone that worked with carpets and linoleum installations. Soon our design pattern and quality of product was chosen and our kitchen received a major facelift makeover! The floor turned out beautiful! A subfloor was purchased also for the whole kitchen and our squeaky floor was GONE! Thank you, GOD, Randall and, the government for making this possible!

Now as we were a low income family, our furniture and assets were mostly from second hand stores. Our gold color couch and dark green embossed window coverings, with distinctive wall pictures and coffee table trinkets, were beautiful, but however, dated.

Our older home now was the recipient of a beautiful new kitchen flooring that shone brightly! The background was a soft matted white with 10 inch soft blue and soft pink square lines. The rest of the kitchen had brown wall paneling and plywood cupboards.

Almost immediately after the flooring was installed, I got great ideas to complete the kitchen's decor with a little bit of painting!

As in the past of Randall's and my relationship, Randall was again about to show great love for me through his acceptance of my sometimes wild ideas. At the time of redecorating, I had absolutely no idea just how strange this particular idea was, at least not until it had been completely carried out and finished!

My favourite color was not just one color but actually the colors of a rainbow, hence, the end product of the cupboards. The pastel pink and pastel blue within the new flooring spurred me to believe that pastel pink and pastel blue cupboards would somehow be enchanting to the eye of every person that came through our back door. Thus matching our floor perfectly!

So with a little, gentle persuasion to my loving Champion in my young life, my professional auto body mechanic and painter, we decided to buy pink and blue cupboard paint! We decided to paint the brown wall panelling a nice clean white to give the illusion of a larger more modern kitchen space. With great enthusiasm, we put on our painting clothes and dug in.

The cupboard doors were taken off of the wall and separated from the backs of the cupboards. Since Randall was the professional painter, he first sanded all the parts and then painted the doors of the cupboards the pastel pink, inside and out. Next, the back and sides of the cupboards were painted the pastel blue. Yikes, this was exciting!

My old, squeaky, dull kitchen was being transformed right before my eyes! How wonderful is that!

Meanwhile, as Randall was dealing with the cupboards project, I was preparing the surface of the wall panelling for its white coat of paint also. It took a couple of weeks to take care of all the painting details, but when all was said and done, no one, anywhere had a kitchen like ours! I guess because of the newness and freshness of every corner and wall, I was totally delighted! In my eyes, even the bold, color of the cupboards, were extremely beautiful!

Looking back almost twenty years into that time frame of 1992, I see me as a young remarried, extremely timid mother of four, that for the first time now, at thirty three years old, an opportunity to express my individual likes and dislikes and not be scorned with violent ridicule.

My dear loving new spouse always treated me with sincere respect with his words and actions alike, as though I was always "his princess".

Thank you Jesus for one of your born again children to walk through life with me as my husbandly "Prince." Your Word say's that you have plans for your children for "Goodness" and to prosper them throughout life. For your promises in scripture, I say, "thank you".

Glory be to GOD, our Yahweh, for ALL "Good things" come from GOD! Thank you, Father.

Yes, our kitchen was on the somewhat radical side of things, but until we moved from that home on Seventh Street, I deeply appreciated the gift of love and acceptance from Randall and my children to explore my heart of hidden desires.

Kitchen
Reflections
of Love

Stop, look and listen,
My sweetheart is in the kitchen,
Supper going strong,
As my sweetheart sings a song.
Every item blended,
Is a treat made with love.
Stirring and tasting,
Adding a few drops from above.
A sprinkle of this,
A sprinkle of that.
Oh, only if he knew,
His special touch of giving,

TRIUMPHANT INNOCENCE

Makes my love for him shine through.
GOD Bless you, Special Partner.
My love for you is real.
I want you to know,
My heart you did steal.
Thank you, Love you Forever!

Chapter Twenty-Six
Some of the Frilly Glue that Holds Our Marriage Together

Morning is here. It's almost time to get up. Randall's side of the bed is empty and it's only 5:00 a.m. Randall has always been a very early riser. He usually is out of the house for a social cup of coffee by 6:00 a.m., except Sunday's. Those day's he might sleep in until 6:00 a.m., if he really tries hard, then at 8:30 we would go to church, for 9:00 o'clock service.

Soon my alarm clock sings as it rings. It is now 7:00 a.m. and it is my turn to get up. Jesus gave me my caring sweetheart, Randall and with Randall, GOD also gave me a new sweet song in my heart.

Many mornings, I would get up and make my way to the washroom and then to the kitchen.

Along the way, many times a week, I would find taped to the bathroom mirror or wedged into the kitchen cupboard and sticking out, a love note from my early riser "Prince Charming."

The notes were usually short, but always tender love wishes for me to have a beautiful day. Sometimes he would wish me safe travels and tell me how much he loves me. Sometimes Randall would write down that he had watched me lay, breathing gently, beside him in the soft blue hue of our night light.

He would wish me luck in anything that I may have been pursuing to do that new day. He was so unselfish about himself!

He adorned me with emotional crowns of adoration and praise, no matter how plain of a woman I am.

Never before had I seen such a giving, caring man! Such tender gentleness from the man I loved was like a Supernatural LOVE bandage from GOD, that soaked my wounded heart, that was fractured and torn from years earlier in my life.

The love notes were a direct line from Randall's heart to the centre of my heart.

Randall's efforts to pursue me in this great way cultivated much passion between us. Because of Randall's persistence, gentle words and behaviour towards me, both of us were abundantly filled with a physical and emotional connection, which I believe is very rare between married couples and sometimes is only read about in romance novels of fiction.

This, almost "supernatural love blessing", I do not take any credit for. I had never been taught how to love, without fear. I had never seen a proper, healthy love relationship in my growing up years. In my first marriage, before Randall, I had suffered critically from lack of love, which now I know as spousal emotional abuse.

I desperately wanted and needed to be loved! But actually, I had become deeply afraid to allow myself to return the endless bond of true love, back to Randall, just in case I would lose my unconditional loving lover, sometime in my future. Was it safe to love unconditionally without hesitance? Was I going to expire if I gave back ALL of my heart to a man that always emptied his whole heart's love in me?

That fear of loss was buried so deep in the cracks of my shattered young heart, that it took Randall almost fifteen years, maybe even longer, for me to unconditionally accept, trust and return my total love to the man GOD sent me.

But as GOD and Randall would have it, the notes kept appearing in numerous locations throughout our home. Love was spread throughout our everyday lives, in gentle touches, whispers and laughter. Randall told me in all different ways how much he loved me by speaking soft words, by the written word, throughout encouraging gestures and always with praises of respect for all that my thoughts and intentions were.

There was no other explanation! My husband wanted me to know that I was his, "Princess" and that he planned on crowning me with the highest form of caring that he could possibly achieve.

For that I am eternally indebted and grateful to the greatest man I have ever met, Randall, my soul mate lover.

Thank you Jesus, for healing my broken heart by giving me the purest love I have ever experienced.

Chapter Twenty-Seven
Hot Is the Word!

Over the many wonderful years that Randall and I enjoyed each other's company, we also enjoyed many frugal holiday excursions.

When our children lived with us, we were owners of a 1979 Dodge Travel, army green van, which took our whole family on quite interesting holidays!

Later in our marriage, we invested in a 1981, GMC, Safari, two toned, red and silver van. It was not a camping van, but we were able to take out the back two seats and back bench seat, therefore making it possible to sleep within the back area.

We bought our Safari van with the mileage readout at 200,000 kilometres and we drove it for several years bringing that mileage reading up to almost 400,000 kilometres, before we sold it. As amazing as it was, every vehicle that we purchased in our first fifteen years of marriage had at least 200,000 kilometres on the odometer before we started driving them. And as amazing as it was, each vehicle was extremely reliable for us, seeming to not want to leave us! They just kept on running and running!

With buying each, much, much older, gently broke in car, truck or van, they were cheaper and we also were able to purchase them with totally loaded electrical packages. Power seats, power windows, air conditioning, velvet interiors, and many other intricate, slightly worn, delicacies were ours to enjoy.

I trusted Randall's car judgement and in turn, both Randall and I were rewarded by GOD. Jesus gave us the "best" of the car "oldies!"

Thanks be to GOD, for Randall's discernment concerning each of our previously owned vehicles! Again, Jesus provided a way, when financially we had very little. But with little, we had much and for that we are very grateful!

Now with our old, faithful red and silver, Safari van, we took it on many trips far and near. As life would have it, one summer, Randall and I, decided to cruise the province of British Columbia with it and use the back of it as our bed and breakfast area.

With great excitement, the van was packed with clothes, bedding, food and drink. As the summer weeks unfolded quickly before our holiday, it wasn't long and it was our time of departure. The summer was an extremely hot wave of air, but none the less, our vacation intentions were kept strong.

We did have air conditioning on the front dash of our van, but never, ever realized the extent of the terrible heat that we were about to endure!

Our holiday departure day came, and Randall and I were off and driving once more, down the Canadian, Number One Highway for our summer vacation. The BC Mountains were our intended destination, mainly Kimberly, the little German town, and Fort Steele, the little historic frontier amusement Fort.

Our reliable, older, well used, Safari, van was as every other summer get away, again getting us from point A to point B and to point C, very well. As usual, Randall and I seemed to almost always conduct our best, one on one, with GOD in the middle, conversations as we drove.

The miles traveled up the road almost seemed to dissolve, as we were lost in deep conversation. Like always, on trips like this one, Randall and I would end up planning sometimes for an hour, more events that where pending on our hearts desires door. As we would drive, we would take hours out of our driving day to plan, explain, and explore each other's ideas for our lives future explorations.

With this pleasing conversation habit, many wonderful GOD blessed adventures unfold almost every time we travel the highways. Because of each of these beautiful closeness times together, our wedded joys grow with every moment we spend time traveling together, side by side.

And yes, now even that over twenty years of marriage have passed, the adventures brought into our lives by current vehicle conversations still draw us together as one, just as GOD intended.

Thank you, Jesus, for my soul mate and earthly best friend, husband and lover! Only through you could such blessings be found, multiplied and deepened.

As we got to our destination, Fort Steele, B.C., the sun was still high in the sky as the temperature was a teetering 37/38 C. Our time of arrival was close to 2:00 p.m., early afternoon.

While looking over towards the treed horizon, blistering hot air was tainted dark blue, with the aroma of smoke from, distant and nearby, forest fires.

As we drove up to the campground reservation cabin and gift store outlet, we noticed an array of heavily populated fifth wheel trailer units that were large. Actually, many, very large, pull type units, side by side throughout the populated trees and sheltering green forest brush filled the camp ground to overflowing! Many of the license plates were from the USA and also from all across the Canadian provinces.

We pulled up to the reservation and campsite store to reserve a camp stall for us and our van. Then, as we walked through the wall of heat from the van to the store office, the hair on our heads dripped with droplets of sweat and moisture. Our clothing clung to us as though someone had just poured liquid from the inside out. We felt like we were melting and decided that we were in great need of at least a small ice cream and a tall can of a cold beverage, if one was available!

Inside we felt the cool, comfortable scented air of the log cabin's air conditioner, with many, "For Sale" items placed throughout many isles of souvenir trinkets. For a precious short time, we lingered and lingered, almost avoiding the fact that, yes we had to brave the antagonising hot outdoors once again!

Then when the camp site reservations were made and ice cream in hand, we headed for the campsite. We would have to come back to browse the Trinkets sections again later and maybe, just maybe, purchase a keepsake for our very own.

Our camping stall was surrounded by a beautiful hedge of young and mature leaf trees. And yes the sun was beating down on everything in a very HOT way. There was NO air breeze, only stifling HOT, Melting, bright sunshine heat.

We exited our vehicle and set up camp. There were no showers, so cooling off in a shower was not possible, but walking back to the camp office that had air conditioning was a possibility. So, slowly but surely, we walked through and around parked trailers, vehicles and wilting trees, back into a heavenly haven of coolness.

With trinkets and more ice bought, we scurried back to our campsite to save the ice from melting right before our eyes.

As the sun lowered in the sky, evening was soon upon us, but the heat was still intolerable! The temperature had to be close to 40 Celsius and we had nowhere to turn for relief.

The van's dash air conditioner was totally useless! The windows in the passenger van could only be pushed out about an inch on each side and back door. As hot and as bad as it was, the hot tainted smoky air penetrated our nostrils leaving our energy to totally ebb out. GOD, help us, please!

As I look back at this particular vacation get-a-way, I have to think seriously that GOD has a sense of humour.

This I believe because as I look back during the middle of that incredibly hot night time sleep event, any one witnessing Randall and I would indeed have had a good belly laugh!

In the dark of the night in hours of extreme heat, Randall and I lay motionless, side by side in the back of our very close quarters van's make-shift bed. If I would barely move a finger, my whole head and body would break out in pouring sweat! Randall had to close the side and back windows because the swarm of mosquitoes was of great invasion!

Between the mosquitoes and fire hot heat, we lay there bare butt naked, motionless and completely helpless in such circumstances! Randall even went outside with two swim towels, dunked them in drinking water and returned to me with them dripping wet to lay them directly on top of us! With only about a thread of air between us, I made it VERY clear..."DO NOT TOUCH ME!!!" And he didn't!

Man, it was HOT!

So, that is how the evening and night unfolded; me, under a wet warmish towel and Randall, silently enduring the same, with a wet warmish towel of his own.

The rest of this particular holiday turned out to be extremely hot throughout our whole time in the mountains as we traveled from campground to campground. It turned out to be a very significant year of heat and fires throughout British Columbia and because of that, it seemed that we turned our future summer vacations towards Saskatchewan sights and sounds. Go figure?

Chapter Twenty-Eight
Down for the Count

Thursday morning at 8:00 a.m., the alarm went off. I got up, went to the living room, turned on the TV and stumbled into the kitchen to get a cup of warm coffee.

Coffee brewing and TV blaring, I went back into our bedroom to get dressed.

Now it was the beginning of May 2007 and I was scheduled to be at my Nanny/housekeeper position by 11:00 a.m. that day. What unfolded over the next 72 hours was nothing short of terrible, crazy and yet full of compassionate people.

When I returned to our bedroom I got out my clothes from the closet, put them on the end of the bed and then sat down on the left side of the mattress. Somewhat a bit stiff and ridged, I was able to get socks and underwear out of the dresser drawer. As I was sitting on the edge of the bed I put my right ankle on top of my left knee. Still my back and body felt tight.

There I sat, left foot on the floor and right leg crossed over on my left leg.

I took my sock and proceeded to bend forward as best as I could, reaching and slipping the sock onto my foot.

With great difficulty I made the attempt. Suddenly without any notice, I heard a very loud "POP" come from my lower back!

WOW!... I couldn't believe the pain!!

I jerked, inhaled and caught my breath! Automatically my reflexes straightened my right leg and I just sat motionless.

There I sat with my back riveted with unbearable sensations of pain throbbing up and down my spine. When I caught my breath, I stood my body up, grabbed the phone beside my bed and very slowly made my way around the bottom end of the bed towards my side of the mattress.

With great effort I gently lowered my injured back slowly into a lying down position and there I lay, one sock on and one sock off.

I couldn't believe what had just happened! In less than a minute I had become completely immobilized!!

My mind was racing...GOD what should I do now?? I have to go to work! I can't move!! The doors are locked!! I need help!! What about my boss?? Who's going to babysit my charges! This morning I have a doctor's appointment! However, I can't move!! Oh dear GOD help me!! Please!

Instinctively, I said an earnest prayer and my mind seemed to somewhat clear. Panic subsided and within moments of asking Jesus for HIS presence and guidance, it seemed I knew what steps I should follow.

Randall had carpooled to work this morning, therefore meaning I couldn't ask him to come home early. He was twenty five miles away at his work site, with no way to get home to me until 5:00 p.m.

As I lay there the pain was ebbing, but as I tried to move my legs the consequence was futile! Laying there motionless I realized, thank goodness, that I had the phone. Thank you Jesus!

First thing I needed was to have something to eat. Who could I call to help me?

I thought of a few people, but this was, Thursday, a work day and my friends had work to be at also.

It was now 8:30 a.m. and I was locked tightly inside our home and had no way to get to the front door to unlock it. I needed someone to get inside to help me so I decided to call Lynn, a close friend of ours. She worked shift work and irregular hours. Hopefully she wasn't at work so I could reach her by phone.

In the middle of everything, I also realized that I was in desperate need to go "number one" but that wasn't going to happen any time soon, at least not in our bathroom!

It was now 8:40 and Lynn answered her phone. I told her of my unscheduled predicament and asked her if she would be able to scout out a lock smith and bring him to our home so she could get inside to me. I let her know also that I very badly needed a bed pan and when I locate one, I'll let her know, so she can pick it up.

Off the phone with Lynn, I was then onto the next call: that being a local pharmacy. By the grace of GOD, when I inquired of the clerk about a bed pan, the answer was, "Yes, there is one pink plastic one left".

I made arrangements with the clerk for Lynn to make a pick- up of the toiletry and then relayed the message to Lynn via phone.

By 9:15 my rescue team had been initiated into action, that being Lynn and locksmith and potty. Now I had to call my boss. Oh dear GOD, I am so sorry for being held up and hurt! But I had to call...

Now the way I look at things is...if you have a job to do, then do it always the best you can as if doing it for GOD, your Father. So for me to call into work to say that I couldn't make it in was harder than hard. However, I had tried intermittently to regain mobility, but was totally unsuccessful in the attempts.

Flat on my back, one sock on, one sock off, I made the dreaded call.

It was now 9:30 and I still hadn't eaten since last night supper and it was time for my confession of distress to my boss, Sarah.

On hearing a "Hello" on the other end of the phone, I blurted out words that sounded somewhat like this: "Hello Sarah. It's me Elizabeth. I can't believe what has just happened! I am and have been lying motionless on my bed since 8:15 am. I've tried moving my legs and body but nothing works!

I am in extreme pain when I try to move my legs and body! I am confined, almost paralyzed with no escape remedy insight!"

Then more urgent words fell from my lips: "I can't come into work! I want to come, but there is no way to get off my bed!" "Please forgive me!"

Now, my boss, Sarah is a very educated yet compassionate employer. Her reaction was not one of panic, but more of reality, care and understanding.

I'm sure this toxic news of distress was a huge inconvenience for her and her husband, because for the last four years they had counted on me to be a reliable employee, which I took very seriously! But now, my respect and dedication for my boss, Sarah and John, her husband, was about to increase even more!

At first the phone went blank. She was a bit stunned with shock, but with a sixth sense, eased into the next sentence.

Soon I was being told that I should take care of my back today and call her back tomorrow, that being Friday. Not to worry, just get better.

My GOD is a good GOD for all the special people that HE has brought into my life over the last 22 years and my employers, Sarah and John, were two of those people! Thank you, Sarah and Jesus.

Done with informing my boss, now back to my emergency.

My doctor's appointment had been scheduled for 10:00 a.m. and it now was 9:45. I dialled again, this time trying to make new arrangements with the clinic.

"Hello, Patsy." I said to the doctor's nurse on the other end. I reported my situation and asked what should I do about my 10:00 o'clock scheduled B12 injection?

Patsy listened intensely. Then she offered for my doctor to come to my rescue at my house!

Again, only compassion and caring surrounded me!

Then Patsy remembered that there was a division of the health system that would be able to deliver my needs, if I needed home care.

Immediately I agreed on contacting the nursing service because I in no way wanted to put my doctor out of her way! Because Jesus gave me a very special GOD loving female Doctor I did not want to over use my privileges with her. I didn't want to take her away from her office and patients.

I was then given the out-patient medical phone number and once again I was organizing my day via my lofty mattress.

It was 11:00 already when I consciously realized that I hadn't eaten since last night supper time. I didn't know if I would have a negative response to not eating regularly and I didn't have any idea when the next morsel of food would come my way.

Randall wouldn't be home for another seven hours and there was no word from Lynn yet, re: the break-in.

I just continued making my phone calls as I saw needed. Thank GOD my mind was bell clear and everything was unfolding well, considering my condition.

As I tried to reach the medical station, there were some difficulties and I was asked to phone different offices. I listened and did just as I was told including checking back to my Doctor's office. The hours seemed to ebb away. Soon it was 12 noon and still no friend, Lynn at my door. By this time all I could think of was my full bladder, motionless body and hungry tummy. 1:00 p.m. rolled around and I was still alone.

I could lightly hear talking coming from the living room television set. You know the old saying: The lights are on, but nobody is home! Well, I now have a new view of that! Boy, if I had been a little fly on the wall, I certainly would have seen it all!

Laying and waiting patiently, I heard a slight noise was coming from what seemed like the front door! Outside was a nice young lock smith, who probably thought a decrepit old lady was locked in this little yellow house. With him was my dear friend, Lynn, by his side carrying the pretty little pink, plastic bed-pan. Finally my rescue had arrived!

I yelled as loud as I could, to signal life to them from the girth of my bed. Faintly I heard a yell back!

Thank GOD! 1:15 and they had finally come!

The lock and door frame seemed to make sounds of resistance, which seemed to be ongoing. Then with a burst of accomplishment my friend broke her way in. I was saved!

Lynn come into my bedroom, over beside my bed and said: "We finally made it! Look at you!"

I asked her then to retrieve my cheque book from a close by cupboard in the room and asked how much do I owe him? With new knowledge, I made out a $65.00 cheque, groaned a sigh of relief, gave her the money and then waited patiently while she went to pay the locksmith.

On Lynn's return we had a short conversation concerning coffee and toast and soon I was munching on freshly buttered brown toast with a pink straw in a cup of coffee. Now that was GOOD!

By now, thirst and hunger taken care of, it was now time for some kind of washroom event. Lynn became my temporary nurse, this time welding the pretty pink plastic user friendly bathroom asset. I had to pee so badly that considering everything else that had transpired so far, this couldn't be that bad, could it?

With great intentions, the episode of going to the potty, was soon done and was all behind me, at least for now, even though peeing uphill was a challenge!

I felt like a new person! I was fed, watered and relieved! Even though I couldn't move, I certainly felt better.

An hour had gone by and Lynn had to get on with her day as well. She left and I was on the phone again, this time finishing making arrangements for my B12 injection.

It wasn't too long and a nurse was at my bedside administering to my medical needs. When all was said and done, I survived the first nine hours and Randall was on his way home.

Soon Randall was at my side and like the prince he is, he had in tow two mama burgers and two vanilla milkshakes, one for him and one for me! Then Randall brought me my laptop hence I already had the phone. He brought me a couple of snacks and the day's newspaper. There in all my glory, I laid and laid some more.

My spirit was anxious to get up and go, but my dilapidated back said: "NOT a Chance!" Therefore, with that said, most of the next three days I just slept and slept some more. I wasn't even able to bend my knees or turn from side to side. Basically, my body and I were forced to be motionless. Yes, that was difficult!

The next day was Friday. Randall didn't go in to work so he could take care of me and do some of his own work. My sweet husband had car things to take care of also, so periodically my prince popped into the bedroom to make sure all was well with me.

I was very concerned, still about going to work and just like yesterday, I was still very laid up! My spirits were extremely low as I had felt like a complete failure to Sarah, my boss. My back was so painful when I tried moving a leg or stretching to turn a bit, that I really didn't know for sure if I would ever walk again!

Friday, 8:00 a.m. came and I had another call to make, this time to report my condition to my employer, like she had asked of me the day before.

In my mind's eye I felt like such a huge disappointment to Sarah that I made my mind up to call her and resign. I just couldn't disappoint her anymore! With tears in my eyes and a shaking voice I called and forced myself to utter words of resignation.

Hardly a moment passed over the open line and the words I heard were so compassionate, tender, firm and sincere that I couldn't stop the tear drops and broken voice sobs.

My dear, sweet boss, Sarah, without any hesitation comforted me with steadfast words that said: "Elizabeth, people make hard decisions when they are in pain. Take it easy and heal your back. We will be ok until you get better. We want you to come back. We don't want anyone else. And don't worry about us, ok? We'll manage."

Never have I met, let alone worked for such caring, loving people. I felt her compassion so strongly that all I could do was say, "Thank you." She wouldn't even listen to my resignation. Thank you, Jesus for such wonderful people in my life.

Sarah then told me to call her sometime next week to keep her updated and with that I replied, "Thank you from the bottom of my heart and yes, I'll keep you posted." When I got off of the phone, all I could do was cry with relief, peace and gratitude.

There I lay, my body motionless but my mind replenished after an emotional conversation and a good night's rest. Randall was in and out all day long, dealing and wheeling also trying to sell my car and do oil changes on our other cars. I think, for Randall, the highlight for him of me being bedridden came on my second day indoors.

While Randall was out, the Hamburger supper from the night before had digested. In the last 10 hours I had been able to use the plastic latrine by myself. However, in transit from chair to my bottom and back, the poor thing had split and was now cracked down the middle! This however didn't deter my usage of it because when I had to go, I HAD to go!

The cavity of the used bedpan had layers of Kleenex piled gently inside, layer after layer.

Randall was gone when the digested last night meal wanted out. I had no alternative. It was now or never, in the bedpan or in the bed. Jesus, please help me!

Still unable to turn or move, I stretched my arm out and reached beside my bed. There the bedpan was sitting on a chair and with great hesitation I lifted it, then, hoped and prayed for it to land in the correct position, under my buttocks.

Duty done, I tried desperately to once again stack the disturbing bed-pan again beside me on the chair. Not liking much of what was happening, success loomed as I piled more Kleenexes over the mess as I hoped for the aroma to be stunted.

With great agony, I have to report that this upsetting scenario, with a cracked pink bed-pan, occurred two more times before my male nurse, Randall, came home from the Health store. With great embarrassment, and disgust, I not only laid there feeling silly as heck, but that is also when Jesus seemed to become "very present" to me.

It was just like, all of a sudden, it seemed like invisible Jesus was sitting in the chair next to my head where the stench package was. He seemed to have a smile on his face and just seemed so relaxed, almost like He found a bit of humour in what He was watching unfold. It was as though He was just letting me know that all was well because He was right beside me and that His Word is true, "I will Never Leave you nor forsake you."

With seeing GOD, in my spirit, His calmness, smile and sense of humour, I also felt like chuckling...a bit. The apparent situation slightly hit my funny bone, because, face it, I was in quite a dilemma predicament.

Poor Randall! He didn't know what was waiting for him here at home! There was not a single thing I could do about the situation, so I quietly giggled and then picked up the phone before he arrived home.

"Hi Honey. Before you come home I just thought I'd let you know that you should please bring some rubber gloves home. I think we'll need some. I love you. See you soon."

Randall was also trying to locate and pick up a metal bed-pan, because I still didn't know how much longer I would be in bed or how much longer the plastic one would last. For now however, the very disturbing broken pan beside me had provided an emense service!

Stacked beside me on a kitchen chair was my Kleenex piled tall, highly aroma substance and now I was getting another strong feeling to release more. I can't tell you how carefully with great calculated accuracy I once again reached for my bathroom fixture, awkwardly placed it, as best as I could, underneath me and proceeded to do my duty.

This truly had to be a GONG show! I couldn't believe this real life situation that I had been thrust into! There was no pride, nor dignity looming. It was all or nothing! I was between a rock and a hard place! And my poor sweetheart was my appointed nurse! Oh, my dear Randall!

With the pan placed back on the chair, I knew it was time to rest.

About an hour had passed by when I heard our back door unlock and open. From the living room, I heard Randall yell at me, "WHAT happened?! Did you throw up!!??", as he was walking towards our bedroom. He entered the doorway and all I could say was, "I guess you could say I did, but not with my mouth!"

The room went silent. Randall seemed to be gasping for breath. I don't think he knew what hit him! There I was laying, still helpless, but with a bit of a mess and nobody to clean it up.

This is when my loving husband kicked into gear and did what no husband should EVER have to do...

He replaced my broken bed-pan with the new metal one, emptied and threw out all aroma debris. He cleaned up his helpless wife and yes, he was ever grateful for the box of plastic surgical gloves!

At that time of our marriage we had been married 16 years and again, like many times in the past, he proved beyond a doubt his unconditional love for me. I love him so much I can't even put it into words.

Thank you, Jesus for blessing and giving me my best friend, Randall, soul mate. I am forever grateful!

As I awoke on the third day, that being Saturday, I noticed that I could move my body and legs some. It had been extremely difficult to lift my upper body until now and completely impossible to sit upright. I was so tired of being forced into the same bed position for the last three days and nights, that on the third day I gave my best laboured try to rise upright with my legs dangling beside the bed.

With great agony...I did it!! Yes, I did it!

My back was starting to heal! I was some dizzy along with extremely weak but, did it ever feel good to rise up from a horizontal position!

By the Grace of GOD the Father, His Holy Spirit and the Love of Jesus, I was on the mend. I was off work for a couple of weeks but believe me, being active once again truly was appreciated by me and my husband, and still is!

Stiff and sore I went back to work but my heart was full of love and appreciation for the family that had, in their way, adopted me. I will always be in their debt for the caring words and actions while always, very eagerly I serve them the best that I am able.

GOD is GOOD! He is apparent in our lives by the people He puts in our lives and the Grace that surrounds us in every situation, good or bad.

Chapter Twenty-Nine
In Appreciation

When Jesus comes into your life, your life will never be the same or boring. When GOD brings your true love partner into your life, you will soar like an Eagle. When we sow seeds of patience, kindness and compassion in our everyday lives, GOD rewards us with the same type people. When we as Christ Believing people strive and serve truth, GOD will ALWAYS be there to meet us!

Sometimes we face hard or terrible situations, people and places within our borders, but Jesus says almost 400 times in HIS Holy Love letter to us, "Do NOT Fear", "I will be with you". When we have to make hard decisions and engage in hard circumstances, Jesus is Faithful to see us through every difficult situation that comes our way!

When we become Born Again Christians, sometimes the faces of the people in our lives change and are replaced by the people GOD wants in our lives. GOD has a future for us, to prosper us and not to harm us.

Because GOD is All Truth, All Righteousness, the Beginning and the End, GOD cannot lie. He therefore proves to be what He says He is.

For over 2000 years GOD's promises have proven true for Saints around the world, even in the darkest moments. When we are down and out, take heart and reach up to the Most High and I guarantee you that HE will take your hand and pull you gently but firmly, out of whatever black pit you may be in.

GOD is bigger than drug dependency, alcohol abuse, nightmares, poverty, a loveless marriage, sickness, unforgiveness, and hatred and, yes, loneliness.

No matter how big your giant is, GOD is Bigger and All powerful!

Before I end my little book of love and romance, I would just like to share a precious scripture that

GOD shared with me by putting on my heart, in the shower, as I was preparing to go to my GOD's house for a Church service and book signing.

In my heart and mind, the scripture: Proverbs, Chapter 3, verses 3 through 10, sums up, in a nut shell, the whole Bible. This is what it reads. Please, trust GOD and claim these verses as your own. Tune into the Light as I believe Jesus is talking to each one of HIS Children.

3. "Let not kindness and fidelity leave you; bind them around your neck;

4. "Then will you win favour and good esteem before GOD and man.

5. Trust in the Lord with all your heart, on your own intelligence rely not;

6. In all your ways be mindful of Him, and He will make straight your paths.

7. Be not wise in your own eyes, fear the Lord and turn away from evil;

8. This will mean health for your flesh and vigour for your bones.

9. Honour the Lord with your wealth,
   with first fruits of all your produce;
10. Then will your barns be filled with
    grain, with new wine your vats will
    overflow.

If you don't know Jesus yet as your personal friend and Saviour, maybe then, now is your special divine appointment to have your name written in the Book of Lambs. This book is a Heavenly book that only GOD knows.

When we ask Jesus into our hearts and ask HIM to forgive us, all our sins, big or little, then the angels of Heaven sing choruses of rejoicing song and your name is written within those very special pages unto Eternity, which is, everlasting Life! Our sins are washed away, forever! No matter what evil we have committed. No matter what our past is, Jesus is now our GOD and mediator who represents us to our Daddy, Father GOD of the Universe.

When you have made a decision to follow Jesus, the Bible says to confess your Salvation with your mouth. Tell a friend, your mother, your father, or a sibling what you have just done and know beyond a doubt that you are now, "Born Again". You are a member of Heaven and Earth!

Now open a Bible. Read and learn exactly what GOD wants you to know about HIM and what He wants for YOU! Feed your spirit, mind and soul to be strong in the name of Jesus! Every promise is there for you to receive and have as your own because GOD is Love and GOD loves YOU! If you were the only person on Earth, GOD would have still sent HIS son, Jesus to die just for you!

Look and reach up, for there you will find Glorious Eternity with Heaven's benefits starting here on Earth immediately!

GOD be with you all, in all you do and say. May your life be healed and true love is poured into your relationships as you soar, day by day, into the Grace, Peace and Love of Jesus Christ, our Heavenly Father and His Holy Spirit!

GOD Bless you always!

In Jesus' Mighty Name!!

Lottie Gillmore

183

CPSIA information can be obtained at www.ICGtesting.com
Printed in the USA
LVOW092314220212

269972LV00004B/3/P

9 781770 694439